Roland's Horn

Also by Marina Tsvetaeva in Christopher Whyte's translations

Moscow in the Plague Year (Archipelago)
Milestones (Shearsman Books)
After Russia (The First Notebook) (Shearsman Books)
After Russia (The Second Notebook) (Shearsman Books)
Youthful Verses (Shearsman Books)
Head on a Gleaming Plate (Shearsman Books)
The Scale By Which You Measure Me (Shearsman Books)

Marina Tsvetaeva

Roland's Horn

Poems 1917–1925

translated from the Russian by
Christopher Whyte

Shearsman Books

First published in the United Kingdom in 2025 by
Shearsman Books Ltd
PO Box 4239
Swindon
SN3 9FN

Shearsman Books Ltd Registered Office
30–31 St. James Place, Mangotsfield, Bristol BS16 9JB
(this address not for correspondence)

EU AUTHORISED REPRESENTATIVE:
Lightning Source France
1 Av. Johannes Gutenberg, 78310 Maurepas, France
Email: compliance@lightningsource.fr

www.shearsman.com

ISBN 978-1-84861-976-0

Introduction and translations
copyright © Christopher Whyte, 2025

The right of Christopher Whyte to be identified as the translator of this work has been asserted by him in accordance with the Copyrights, Designs and Patents Act of 1988.
All rights reserved.

Contents

Introduction   9

MILESTONES 2 (1921)

I

'Darkness, and the whole world starts migrating'   35
'No sooner have my burning eyelids closed'   35
'Darling fellow travellers we shared a'   36
'Bleary-eyed and menacing'   36
'Kissing the brow – puts care to flight'   37
'Mud sputters up'   38
'My spell will conjure you from gold'   39
'I have a story for you of huge fraud'   39
'My steed is a consuming fire!'   40
'Every poem's a child of love'   40
'I'm giving you this comb so you'll remember'   41
'Into this drink I have dissolved'   41
'But on my forehead stars'   42
'My way does not lead past your house'   43
'My bearing's unpretentious'   44
'Hunchbacks, beggars, thieves – I've kissed them all!'   45

II

'And God said'   46
'All you need do is live! – I let my hands'   46
'I stand with head thrown back and lowered eyes'   46
'Flesh for the flesh, for the spirit spirit'   47
'I'm no impostor, I've made my way home'   48
'My darling, you are clothed in rags'   48
'Words are traced out in the nighttime sky'   48
'I bless the labour of each day'   49
'Tears, tears – stream of living water!'   49
'Hands useless to the one we love'   49
'Our two souls are as near'   50

'Knight resembling an angel, Duty!'	50
'Courage, virginity – a combination'	50
'So, tossing my head back'	51
'Bring me what everyone else has no need for'	51
'It's my pleasure to offer an example'	52
'If stanzas cannot help, nor constellations'	52
'Love! Love! Convulsed by spasms, in the grave'	53
'I know I will die at the edge of the day – but at which'	54

UNCOLLECTED POEMS 1920–1925

Lyrics from the Drama 'The Disciple'

1. 'When rolling waves'	55
2. '"Faithful", she says'	55
3. 'I came to you in search of bread'	56
4. 'There, along a rope drawn taut'	56
5. (Sailors and Poets)	57
6. (The Singer – to the Girls)	58
7. 'Dancing round, dancing round'	59
8. 'Parting's your trade. Why should you care'	60
9. 'Last night you gazed into my eyes'	61

To the Jews	63
'Roses will blossom tomorrow'	63
Earthly Name	64
'Sunset's darling blaze was ended'	64
'Though still alive, I fold my arms'	65
'Denying God, the Wandering Jew'	65
'A home at whose door no one knocks'	66
'Just equals, same as yes and no'	67
'If I give somebody my hand'	68
'"How many men do you keep up with?"'	68
'Love, honour – I don't give a damn'	69
'Wind, oh wind that sweeps along'	70
'I picture you with dark eyes – separation!'	70
'Others with eyes and with a brilliant face'	71
'Disappearing into the black night'	72

'June, July – time of warbling nightingales'	72
'<…> if there's nothing to be done'	73
'Down in the basements, windows decked in red'	73
'Like people drinking in deep gulps'	74
'It all over again: once more a shy'	74
'Hear your willing servant, God'	76
'Feats get accomplished. Poems on those death-'	77
The Wolf	78
'Don't tell anyone my name'	79
To an Alien	80
'I know that velvet-like fragility'	81
'"Farewell!" – Splashing across the countryside'	81
'Hair like brief wings, a flurry'	82
'"Was he your husband?" – "No."'	82
The Bolshevik	84
Roland's Horn	85
'Away the path tears'	86
'Competition's scab did not'	86
'Pride and shyness – daughters of one mother'	87
'Not for these flattering vestments, lying cassocks'	87

His Partner

(1) He sleeps, the joy your torment brought'	88
(2) 'Clothed in his infant tears'	89
(3) 'Sweep of an outsize wing'	90
(4) 'How to recompense you, how to help?'	90
(5) 'With him to the end'	91

'Incontrovertible, so simple'	92
'Eyebrows darting leagues apart'	92
'What's this – what wing, what sound'	92
'Acquaintance! Where did you reach these parts from?'	93
'In the chapel they'd'	94
'And you say'	95
'Could these be leaves, falling from trees'	96
'Divine, without restraint'	97
'Imperceptibly the golden'	97

'And what of love? A shepherd lad'	98
'Orphaned air beyond the grave'	98
Asrael	99
'A font for doves'	100
Prague	100
Night	101
Lotus Juice	103
'Just like into the seas' pure blue'	104
'However bitter, gulping down the smoke'	104
'Along the riverbanks, grey trees show where'	105
Eye	106
'You, who loved me with the lie'	106
'Pillars in a throne room that's'	106
'Song from a wound between the prince's ribs'	107
'Not thundering from passing wheels'	107
'Days that resemble crawling slugs…'	107
'Arrogance – a matter of caste'	108
'Fame falls, plopping just like a plum'	108
'From native villages!'	108

from POEMS TO BLOK (1922)

10. 'See him – look there! – grown tired of foreign parts'	111
11. 'For us you will remain a monk'	111
12. 'Friends of his, don't trouble him!'	112
13. 'Over the plains'	113
14. 'It wasn't ribs that cracked'	113
15. 'Without a call, without a sound'	114
16. 'Sleepy, as if drunken'	116
17. 'Therefore, oh Lord! accept my coin'	117

from THE CRAFT (1922)

Bethlehem	
(1) 'Not with silver I came'	118
(2) 'Emperors three'	119
Notes	120

INTRODUCTION

A letter from Tsvetaeva to Yevgeny Lann from the end of December 1920 gives an impression of how she and her eight-year-old daughter Alya lived, once the "plague year" of 1919 and the worst experiences of the Civil War and War Communism were behind them:

> Alya and I are sitting, writing. Evening. A knock at the unlocked door. Me, not lifting my eyes: 'Come in!' A profiteer from the Smolensk market enters. He wants to exchange tobacco for millet. (Fool!) 'This is where you live?' 'Yes.' 'But it's a backyard!' 'A slum,' I correct him. 'Ok, ok, a slum… But earlier you must have…' 'Yes, yes, we haven't always lived like this.' Alya, proudly: 'We had a fireplace burning, and officer cadets sitting round, there was even a poodle – Jack. Once he fell right into our soup.' I, in explanation: 'He ran out onto the attic roof and smashed through the skylight.' Alya: 'And then he got stolen.' The profiteer: 'But how did you end up living like this?' 'Sit down, have a cigarette.' (Forgetting he deals in tobacco. Tactfully, he doesn't refuse.) – 'Stage by stage: to begin with the attic, then a den, then a hovel.' 'Next comes a rubbish heap,' puts in Alya. 'Your daughter's so precocious!' 'She's understood everything since she was one year old!' 'You don't say!' – Silence. – Then: 'Better if I go, I'm sure you have writing to do, I'm disturbing you.' 'For goodness' sake, don't go. I'm so glad to see you, it's obvious you're a good person, and I badly need tobacco!' 'No, it's better if I go.' And me, horrified: 'Maybe you think I don't have any millet? Look – a sack of the stuff!' Alya: 'And we've got more in the pitcher!' 'I see, I see, but your Mum's so absent-minded.' 'She's not absent-minded, she gets carried away, she's always like that!' 'Please, let me take my leave.' Me: 'Listen, you've got tobacco, I've got millet, where's the problem? I can easily exchange it at the

Smolensk market tomorrow, but rather than second-rate tobacco I'll be given rubbish, sawdust. Go on!'

'What price is your millet?'

'Tell me how much you want to give.'

'1,000 roubles?'

'Splendid. And the tobacco?'

'10,000 roubles.'

'Couldn't be better. Take 10 pounds of millet and give me a pound of tobacco.' Alya appears with the scales. We do the weighing. 'But I don't have anything to take it away in.' 'Just take it in the sack...' 'But we don't know each other, and the sack is worth something...' 'The sack isn't worth anything, a human being is. You're a good person, take the sack.' 'Then instead of a pound of tobacco, let me give you a pound and a half.'

'You're making me embarrassed!'

'Please, go on!'

Alya: 'Marina, take it!'

Me: 'You're very kind.'

Him: 'It's the first time I've met anyone like you.'

Me: 'Off their head?'

Him: 'No – normal. I'll take away a troublesome, yet comforting impression.'

'Please, just the latter!'

He smiles. As farewell: 'God preserve you.'

Coming up for 50, could be an exciseman, voice sort of purrs, keeps catching his breath.

The last visitor of the three described in the letter is a people's commissar who comes with rather more disturbing news. The attitude of Tsvetaeva and her daughter is equally unconventional:

> Alya and I are sitting, writing. Evening. The door – no knock – is thrown wide open. A soldier from the commissariat. Tall, thin, Caucasian fur hat. 19 years old.
>
> 'Are you citizen such and such?' 'That's me.' 'I've come to fill in a report about you.' 'Mmh.' Him, thinking

I didn't get it: 'A report.' 'I understand.'

'By leaving the tap on and flooding the blocked sink, you smashed the new cooker in no. 4.' 'In other words?' 'The water, seeping through the ceiling, dislodged the bricks bit by bit. The cooker collapsed.' 'OK.' 'You reared rabbits in the kitchen.' 'That wasn't me, it was someone else.' 'But *you're* supposed to be the householder?' 'Yes.' 'So keeping the place clean is up to you.' 'Yes, yes, you're right.' 'Do you have another storey in the flat?' 'Yes, above us there's a mezzanine.' 'A what?' 'A mezzanine.' '"Meezymim", "meezymim" – how do I write that – "meezymim"?' I tell him. He writes it down. Shows me. And, giving my approval: 'That's right.'

'This is shameful, citizen. You're an intelligent person!' 'That's the whole problem, if I were less intelligent, none of all this would have happened – all I ever do is write.' 'So what do you write?' 'Poems.' 'You compose?' 'Yes.' 'How pleasant.' A pause. 'Citizen, could you check over what I've written?' 'Give it here, I'll write it down, you tell me, and I'll write.' 'It's not nice, writing things about yourself.' 'Makes no difference – it won't take long!' I write. He loves my handwriting: fast and stylish.

'It's easy to see you're a writer. Given you're so capable, why don't you find a better apartment? Forgive the expression, but this – it's a hole in the ground!'

Alya: 'A hovel.'

We write. Put our signatures. He gives a courteous salute, hand to his cap. And disappears.

That evening, half past 10 in the evening – God save us! – he reappears.

'No fear, citizen, we're old friends! Here I am again, just some things we need to sort out.'

'Be my guest.' 'So, I have to trouble you again.'

'I'm at your service. Alya, make space on the table.'

'Perhaps you want to add something in your defence?'

'I can't say… The rabbits weren't mine, the piglets weren't mine – and they've already been eaten.'

'So there were piglets too? We should write that down.'

'I couldn't say… Better add nothing.'

'Rabbits… Rabbits… It must be cold here in your place, citizen. I'm sorry.'

Alya: 'Cold for who? For the rabbits, or for Mummy?'

Him: 'For whoever… Rabbits… They chew everything up.'

Alya: 'They chewed up Mummy's mattresses in the kitchen, and a piglet lived in my bath-tub.'

Me: 'Don't write that down!'

Him: 'I'm sorry for you, citizen!'

He offers me a cigarette. We write. It's already half past 11.

'I'm sure you didn't use to live like this…'

On his way out: 'Either arrest or a fine of around 50,000. I'll come and tell you.'

Alya: 'With a revolver?'

Him: 'Lady, no need to fear that!'

Alya: 'So you can't shoot?'

Him: 'I can, I can, but… I'd be sorry for the citizen lady here!'

After the death in February 1920, in a state orphanage, of her younger daughter Irina, Tsvetaeva was assigned a ration, thanks to which where the next meal was coming from ceased to be a matter of basic survival. The tones of high comedy she uses to describe both encounters ought not to mislead us as to the utter grimness of the underlying reality, or the trauma of the years immediately preceding. A poem dated October 1919 and beginning 'My attic palace, my palatial attic!' offers a consciously idealised depiction of the very same living quarters, claiming that 'angels and demons' are frequent visitors, given that 'it's just a step from heaven to the roof!' The poem's conclusion reverses the direction and implies that the uninterrupted availability of suicide as a possible escape can help to make the situation bearable: 'It's just a step from the roof – into heaven.' Entering heaven is a euphemism for self-immolation.

The years between the twin revolutions of 1917 and Tsvetaeva's departure at the end of April 1922, together with Alya, for Berlin and then Prague were the most productive of her entire career. In addition to a host of shorter, lyrical items, she wrote the long poems *On a Red Steed* and *Tsar-Maiden*, the latter a reworking and reimagining of folklore material in characteristically disconcerting and idiosyncratic style. Thanks to a chance meeting on the train which brought her back from Crimea to Moscow in November 1917, Tsvetaeva became acquainted with Pavel Antokolsky and, through him, with the members of the drama studio run by Yevgeny Vakhtangov, inspiring her to write no fewer than five dramas in verse, *Red Ballet* and *Snowstorm* in 1918, *Fortuna*, *Angel of Stone* and *Phoenix* in 1919. There, too, she met the actor Yury Zavadsky, at the time involved in a gay relationship with Antokolsky, and the diminutive actress with an English surname, Sonechka Holliday, to both of whom she dedicated extended cycles not fully assembled till after her death, as was the cycle of twenty-seven poems addressed to the painter Nikolay Nikolayevich Vysheslavtsev (1890–1952), headed only by his initials.

The contrast between this outpouring of verse, and the circumstances of inconceivable hardship which formed a background, could hardly be more striking. Tsvetaeva commented that

> I didn't mention the most important thing of all: high spirits, clarity of thought, explosions of joy at each minimal piece of luck, everything in me strained to the utmost – the walls are covered with lines of poetry and jottings for the notebook.

A delicious annotation dated October 11th 1918 reads:

> All I need to do is get a bit distracted – for example, while standing in a queue – bow my head – and words start making music.

Another notebook entry describes plans for an essay which, perversely, would have itemised all the benefits deriving from the arrival of the Bolshevik regime:

> I want, in all seriousness, to write an article (the first one in my life – which, when it comes down to it, won't be an article!) – "Justifying Evil" (that is, Bolshevism).
>
> What Bolshevism gave me by depriving me of things.
> (1) Freedom in dressing (the chance to masquerade 24 hours out of 24), of speech (nothing to lose!), dying whenever you choose to (all you need do is walk out into the street and shout: *Vive le roi!*), sleeping the whole night outside – the complete heroic adventure of being poverty-stricken.
> (2) Finally having the right to despise one's friends (the ones who didn't come to my assistance in 1919).
> (3) Finally proving that heaven is worth more than bread (I tested this in person and now I have *the right* to talk this way!)
> (4) The ultimate proof that what brings people together and unites them is not political convictions – under absolutely no circumstances political convictions! (I have wonderful friends among the communists).
> (5) The destruction of the barriers between classes, not through the compulsion of ideas, but through the generalised suffering of Moscow in 1919 – hunger, cold, illnesses, hatred of Bolshevism &c.
> (6) The demonstration of how absolutely genuine my love of my neighbour is (I'm ready to defend any landed proprietor – best of all Nozdrev – he has splendid wooden barrel organs and dogs!)
> (7) Deepening love for everything we've been deprived of (parades, marches past, masquerades, names, medals!)

And at another point:

In the Moscow of 1919, one cannot be surprised at anything: absolutely the right time for me to be alive.

Totting up the shorter poems Tsvetaeva was writing – figures can only be approximate, not least because some items cannot be dated precisely – gives 89 for 1917, 157 (!) for 1918, 76 for 1919, 85 for 1920, 106 for 1921 and 88 for 1922. (For 1923 the figure is 100, for 1924, 21 and for 1925, 13). Yet from 1912, when her third book, *Magic Lantern*, appeared, containing a selection from her first two, until Kostry of Moscow published *Milestones 2* in 1921, not a single book by Tsvetaeva was issued. She would write to Yury Ivask in April 1933 that no fewer than three major collections had fallen by the wayside during this period.

If one reads in chronological order, it is striking to observe the different kinds of poems Tsvetaeva composed, sometimes on the very same day. As a result, when publishing again became feasible, the poet had an enormous range to choose from. Her practice so far had been to present items in strict chronological order. Breaking with that habit, she organised two books thematically, or grouped into cycles. *Youthful Verses*, covering the period from 1913 to 1915, is chronological. *Where Swans Are Camped*, Tsvetaeva's dogged and unapologetic homage to the Whites, the counter-revolutionary forces opposing the Bolsheviks, brings together items written between 1917 and 1920. Neither of these books was to see the light of day during the poet's lifetime. The first was published in Paris in 1976, the second in Munich in 1957. *Psyche*, published by Grzhebin in Berlin in 1923, consists entirely of cycles and has a substantial overlap with other collections, also including work by the poet's daughter Alya.

Milestones 2 appeared in advance of the first *Milestones*, in an edition disfigured by errors Tsvetaeva is said to have corrected painstakingly by hand, in copy after copy, then in a second, improved edition from the same publishing house in 1922. In that year the Moscow State Publishers brought out the first *Milestones*, while in Berlin two slim volumes appeared with the *Poems to Blok*, then *Separation*, which included 'On a Red Steed'. *Tsar Maiden* was published both in Moscow and, in a slightly altered second edition, with Epokha in Berlin. The culminating triumph in her reworking of folk-based material, *Molodets* (generally rendered as *The Swain*, though it could also be *The Champion*) came out in Prague in 1924. The two remaining collections Tsvetaeva was to produce in the course of her lifetime, *The Craft* (Berlin 1923) and *After Russia* (Paris 1928) return to chronological presentation.

The most tragic event of these appallingly difficult years was the death from malnutrition, on February 15th 1920 (February 2nd Old Style) of Tsvetaeva's second child Irina, born April 13th 1917, so therefore not quite three years old, in the state orphanage at Kuntsevo outside Moscow. On the advice of an acquaintance, Tsvetaeva entrusted both her children to the institution on November 14th 1919, on the understanding that they would be regularly fed and cared for at a level she herself could not provide. When Alya contracted malaria, her mother brought her home to nurse her. The sequence of events emerges from two letters to Tsvetaeva's actress friend Vera Zvyagintseva (1894–1972). The first, from early on in February, was never posted:

> These last days I felt so happy: Alya was getting healthier, I was writing again, after two months, more and better than ever before. I dashed about singing, flew round the shops – in a state of blessedness! – Alya and poems.
>
> I've put a book together – from 1913 to 1915 – old poems came back to life and resurrected, I improved them and tidied them up, crazily carried away by me at 20 and all the people I loved then: myself – Alya – Seryozha – Asya – Pyotr Efron – Sonya Parnok – my young grandmother – the generals of 1812 – Byron and – there's no counting them!
>
> Then Alya got ill – and I *cannot* write, I'm not entitled to, because it means delight and luxury. So I write letters and read books. From which I draw the conclusion that my only *luxury* is my craft, the one I was born to exercise.
>
> This letter will turn you cold, but understand me: I'm a lonely person – alone under the sky – (since me and

Alya make up one), I have nothing to lose. No-one helps me to live, I don't have a father, or a mother, grandparents or friends. I'm disgracefully alone and therefore entitled to anything. Even to crime!

Since I was born I have been excluded from the *circle of people*, from society. Behind me stands, not a living wall, but a cliff: Fate. I live, spectating life – *all of life* – Life! I don't have an age or a face. Maybe I am Life itself. I'm not afraid of getting old, I'm not afraid of being laughed at, I'm not afraid of poverty, of having enemies, of evil tongues. Beneath my cheerful, fiery exterior, I'm stone, i.e. invulnerable. – I have only Alya. Seryozha. Even if I wake up tomorrow with grey hair and wrinkles – who cares? – I shall create my own Old Age – and nonetheless I was so little loved!

I shall live – others have Lives.

In spite of which, how much delight I got from each blouse of Alya's ironed, each clean plate! – Our ration of bread! And how I'd love to get a new dress!

The following letter, dated Friday February 7th (Old Style, according to the prerevolutionary calendar) brings the horrendous news:

Remember, Verochka, that time in my room, on the couch, I asked you again, and you answered 'Perhaps' – and I cried out in such horror: 'God spare us!' And now it is reality, and cannot be made good. I heard about it *by accident*, I was going to the League for Saving Children on Sobachya Square to find out about a sanatorium for Alya – and all at once: a chestnut-coloured horse and a sled with straw – from Kuntsevo – I recognised them. I climbed up, they called me. 'You Mrs So-and-so?' 'Yes.' And they told me. She wasn't ill, she died from debility. I didn't even go to the burial – that day Alya's temperature was 40.7 – and – want to know the truth? – I just *couldn't*. Dear God! There would be so much to say about this.

All I will say is it's a *stupid dream*, I keep on thinking I'll wake up. At times I completely forget, feel pleased because Alya's fever is lessening, or because of the weather – and all at once – good God in Heaven! – I'm still not able to believe it! I live with clenched throat, on the edge of a precipice. Now I understand so much: it's all the fault of my love of adventure, not taking difficulties seriously, being healthy, in the last analysis, my monstrous ability to cope. When you can handle things, you don't see how hard it is for other people. And – in the last analysis – I was so abandoned! Everyone has someone – a husband, a father, a brother – all I had was Alya, and Alya was ill, and I became totally absorbed in her illness – and God has punished me.

Nobody knows – only a young woman here, Irina's godmother, a friend of Vera Efron's. I told her so she could prevent Vera going sometime to see Irina – everything here was more or less ready, and I had already talked to some woman or other about going to collect Irina for me – it was supposed to happen on Sunday.

Oh!

Please! Tell me something, give me an explanation!

Other women forget about their children due to balls – love affairs – parades – the feastdays of life. My feastday in life is poetry, but that's not what made me forget about Irina – I hadn't written anything for two months! And – it makes my hair stand on end! – I hadn't forgotten her, not for a moment, I kept tormenting myself and asking Alya: 'Alya, what do you think – – –?' And I kept on getting ready to go for her, thinking: 'Now Alya is getting better and I can bring Irina home!' But now it's too late.

Tsvetaeva had last seen her husband Sergei Efron in January 1918, when he made a brief, clandestine visit to Moscow before joining the counter-revolutionary forces. She was long without any news of him, uncertain whether he was alive or dead. In March 1921, Ilya Ehrenburg carried abroad a letter from Tsvetaeva which reached

Sergey in June. In it the poet speaks about Irina's death:

> If you are alive, then the person who will attempt to get this letter to you will describe the exterior circumstances of my life. I can't. It would be too much, and it's not what matters.
>
> If you are alive, then it is *such* a miracle that not one single word should be pronounced, something else is required.
>
> But, so you won't hear the painful news from indifferent lips – Seryozhenka, last year, at the time of the feast of the Presentation, Irina died. Both of them got sick, I *managed* to save Alya, but not Irina.
>
> Seryozhenka, if you are alive, then we will meet, and have a son. Do what I do: *don't* think about it.
>
> Not as a consolation to either you or me, but because it is the plain truth, let me say that Irina was a very strange child, perhaps a hopeless case, all the time she rocked back and forth, she barely spoke. Maybe it was rickets, or else a defect from birth, I cannot tell.
>
> Of course, if the Revolution hadn't happened –
>
> Well – if the Revolution hadn't happened –
>
> Don't mistake my attitude for heartlessness. It's merely a way of surviving. I've turned to stone. I try to turn to stone. The worst thing of all is dreaming. When I see her in a dream – her curly head in that soiled dress – oh, then, Seryozhenka – only death can bring relief. [...]
>
> I'm not going to put down the details of Irina's death for you. That was an *appalling* winter. It's a miracle that Alya survived. I *snatched* her from death, when I myself was totally unequipped!
>
> Don't feel bitter about Irina, you simply didn't know her, imagine that you dreamed it all, don't accuse me of being heartless, I just don't want you to suffer – I take it all upon myself!
>
> We'll have a son, I know we will – a wonder-working, heroic son, seeing both of us are heroes.

Towards the end of August 1916 Tsvetaeva had already composed two poems about having a son. In the first, an eighteen-year-old's brief liaison with an actress produces a son he knows nothing about, 'blissfully unaware that you had sown the seed/ for such beauty', while in the second a woman travelling on a tram studies a teenager close by and imagines how it would feel if she could address him as her 'son'. The near obsession would persist until the birth in February 1925 of Georgy, known in the family after E.T.A. Hoffmann's cat as Murr. The poem entitled 'A Son', dated Easter Monday 1920, addresses this figure directly, concluding:

> Emerging from the watchful shadows
> of the Kremlin's topmost towers,
> in the twilight throng I glimpsed
> one who's still to arrive – *my son*.

An extended section in Tsvetaeva's notebooks deals with the circumstances of Irina's death, under the heading 'The Kuntsevo Epos'. However, in her poetry or in her published work, the topic inspires only one poem, also written on that Easter Monday, which begins 'Two hands, each lowered gently/ onto a young child's head!' and ends 'It's still impossible to grasp/ my child lies in the earth'. The fact can prompt us to reflect on the filters which intervene between Tsvetaeva's actual, lived experience and her poetry. It would be improper to speak of the books where poems are ordered according to the date as lyrical diaries, precisely because the literary work is a transformation and refashioning of lived experience. Automatically reading from one back to the other would be ill-advised.

In the poems of *Milestones 2*, and in the uncollected poems from these years, Tsvetaeva speaks through the voice of a whole range of feminine personae. However passionate and convincing her identification with them may be, it would be unwise to conclude that they reflect her own actions and behaviour. The sexually promiscuous woman ready to sleep with practically any man who presents himself crops up again and again, as in the item which concludes the first half of *Milestones 2*, 'Hunchbacks, beggars, thieves – I've kissed them all!' 'It all over again – once more a shy' is fascinating in several respects. It chronicles the dull, paradoxically repetitive nature of having a series of brief encounters with different men. We have no reason to doubt that the hardship and the breakdown of normal life which characterised the years immediately after the Bolshevik revolution were accompanied by a slackening of conventional sexual morality. To what extent Tsvetaeva herself, rather than merely observing, participated in this remains a moot point. The three involvements which generated the largest body of poetry – with Zavadsky, Holliday and Vysheslavtsev – were all unrequited, or else platonic in nature.

'It all over again – once more a shy' also offers an idea of how Tsvetaeva went about building a poem, through repeated syntactical parallelism, here tellingly mirroring the monotony which is the poem's theme. This creates, so to speak, a series of slots, stanza by stanza, not all of which have been filled out. In terms of tone, there is an uneasy, disconcerting blend of self-abandonment and self-abasement, practically a refusal to care for the self, accompanied by a chill, cynical detachment which conveys a deep, inner conviction of superiority. The speaker concedes and withholds herself at one and the same time. The poem is indicative of how Tsvetaeva challenges gender stereotypes by pushing them to the very limit, as well of a persistent preoccupation with female victimology.

Milestones 2 which, as has been said, was published in advance of the first *Milestones*, brought Boris Pasternak the revelation of Tsvetaeva's poetry. He described the effect it had on him in a verbose, rather pompous letter dated February 10th, 1923, marking the start of a correspondence running to over 200 items which continued until 1935. Mislaid during the war, when Pasternak entrusted them to a woman friend for safe keeping, Tsvetaeva's letters have been reconstructed from the rough copies in her notebooks, and constitute an achievement on the same level as the very best of her poetry. According to Pasternak, while reading aloud to his brother the very last item in the collection, 'I know I will die at the edge of the day – but at which', he was interrupted by his own sobbing. 'I have a story for you of huge fraud' and 'Miles, more miles, stale bread' produced the same effect. The two had walked side by side in the funeral procession for the composer Alexander Scriabin (1872–1915), and Pasternak could not understand why Tsvetaeva had not informed him then of her stature as a poet, leaving him instead to make the discovery years later.

The two parts of *Milestones 2* are distinctly different in tone yet bear markers of the same voice and authorship. The first part is earthy, carnal and transgressive. Gypsies and fortune-tellers put in appearances, as instances of an alternative, non-patriarchal access to knowledge of the future, and of an idealised life beyond the bounds of conventional society, where women and men participate in shared exploits on conditions of near equality. The second part is more spiritual and ethereal, with references to the Bible and churchgoing, to angels and the virtue of virginity, concluding with two splendid anticipations of death in bounding, explosive metres. 'If stanzas cannot help, nor constellations' shows us the poet at work during her beloved nocturnal hours. The rhythm is meditative and hesitant, postponing the answer to a question prompted by the rhyme in Russian between 'constellation' and 'retribution'.

The uncollected poems featured here begin with a series of lyrics from a drama entitled *The Disciple*, which has not survived. *The Craft* contains a sequence of seven powerful poems with the same title, addressed to Prince Sergei Volkonsky (1860–1937), a gay aristocrat whose work Tsvetaeva was to copy out by hand, and who himself later wrote in Paris about their friendship, in illuminating and warmly appreciative terms. The maritime imagery of the uncollected lyrics, however, strongly recalls the poems to Vysheslavtsev. We read in her notebooks:

> I spent the whole day writing: first of all a letter to NN (which I sent through Alya), then *The Disciple* – I wrote an amazing little song, it delights me (as if it were someone else's), with this refrain 'me, carried in no mother's/

womb, but in the sea's'. I have it in the First Act – before going to sleep – the poet disciple, who is totally me.

A manuscript note indicates that the addressee of 'To an Alien' is Anatoly Lunacharsky (1875–1933), Soviet people's commissar from 1917 to 1929, with responsibility for the Ministry of Education. In her memoir 'My Jobs', Tsvetaeva describes her first encounter with Lunacharsky, who was also a playwright, when on July 6th 1919, at the Palace of Arts, she read out the final monologue from *Fortuna*, rejoicing at the opportunity to confront a people's commissar with the words of an aristocrat, only regretting she could not read them out to Lenin, or to the entire staff of the Lubyanka. At the same event, Lunacharsky read his translations of a Swiss poet, Carl Muller. In November 1921, Tsvetaeva was accompanied to the Kremlin by Vladimir Wolkenstein, who has been proposed as the dedicatee of 'Wolf' and who had been briefly married to Sophia Parnok in 1906–1908. Tsvetaeva's passionate liaison with Parnok between 1914 and 1916 is the subject of the 'With a Woman' cycle in *Youthful Verses*. The purpose of the visit was to gain an audience with Lunacharsky, and arrange relief for hungering writers in Crimea. She described the meeting in a letter to Max Voloshin:

> Without realising, I smile! That intoxicating sensation – *en présence de quelqu'un*. Kind eyes. 'Are you here about the hunger in Crimea? I'll do everything!' Me, in an impassioned whisper: 'That's so good of you!' 'Write it, write it down, I'll do everything!' Me, carried away: 'You're an angel!' 'The names, the addresses, what they need, leave nothing out – and don't worry, everything will get done!'

'To an Alien' gives expression to Tsvetaeva's dogged refusal to take sides, to allow basic human solidarity to succumb in the wake of the polarisation which so often follows from ideological conflicts. A similar spirit underlies 'The Bolshevik', addressed to Boris Bessarabov (1897–1970), five years her junior, who had volunteered for the Red Army in September 1919 and who briefly lived with Tsvetaeva and Alya on Borisoglebsky Pereulok. He offered her practical help, but also copied out *Tsar Maiden*, and carried a letter and an icon from her to Anna Akhmatova in St Petersburg. He also inspired a never completed poem about a folk hero, *Egorushka*. This is how Tsvetaeva described him, in another letter to Lann (January 19th, 1921):

> 18 years old. A Communist. No boots. Hates Jews. At the last minute, when the Whites were approaching Voronezh, he joined the party. Not long back from the Crimean front.
>
> Now he lives in a suffocating, half clerical, half intellectual, counterrevolutionary family (household!) – chopping wood, carrying water, shifting bits of furniture that weigh nearly 200 kilos and can't be burned, on Sundays he cleans out the Augean stables (he calls it 'Sunday overtime'), the whole day long he listens to diatribes and snake-like hissing against the Soviet government – listens, with downcast eyes (the marvellous eyes of a three-year-old boy, who has not yet fully woken up!) – having done all the outstanding work in his "commune" (all these words are his!) he goes off to do the same for the Princes Shakhovskoy – listens to the same – to the Scriabins, where he doesn't listen, but each day saws and chops wood for four stoves and a cooker! – (they've put one in at last!) – and for the Zaitsevs and so on – till late at night, not to mention all the effort he puts in to extricate friends, and friends of friends, from problematic situations.
>
> He's taken for a fool. Externally, he's like some "bogatyr" from the folktales. All his cheeks glow raspberry red, a frenzied whirlwind – all his blood is pulsing round! – his hair, great black eyes glistening like jewels, an enchantingly small and innocent mouth, a straight nose, a very pale and high forehead. Massive, well-developed shoulders – an unbelievable match for my Tsar-Maiden!
>
> Everything about him is unusually serious for some-

one just 18. He reads books five times over, hunting for their MEANING, which the author was frivolous enough to forget about, he *respects* art, he'd go through fire and water for the poetry of Tyutchev – the *preferred reading* – for his soul – is fairy stories and heroic tales. He adores fir trees, work, markets, he's delighted that Russia still has 'fine, sturdily built priests' (and doesn't himself believe in God!)

A "bogatyr" is a hero from Russian folk epic. 'Hear your willing servant, God' is placed in the mouth of just such a figure. Evgeniy Lann (1896–1958) arrived in Moscow from Kharkov at the end of November 1920, bringing news of the poet's sister Asya in Crimea. He was the object of a brief infatuation on Tsvetaeva's part lasting barely two and a half weeks which prompted the poems 'Don't tell anyone my name', 'I know that velvet-like fragility' and '"Farewell!" – Splashing across the countryside', as well as the long poem 'On a Red Steed' which would subsequently bear a dedication to Anna Akhmatova. In a letter to Lann dated December 6th 1920, Tsvetaeva writes:

> How strange: I brought everybody happiness! Sometimes ethereal, sometimes piercing – but never a weight that could suffocate! Whereas it seems that I suffocate you. If you only knew how I restrain myself, don't let myself go, minimise, smooth things out, neutralise every look and step!
>
> Thus, bit by bit, arms that were thrown wide to welcome you keep falling, falling, relinquishing and releasing. Oh, for those fallen arms *God will forgive me everything*!

'Roland's Horn' is an emblematic poem, almost a manifesto, on two accounts. It expresses Tsvetaeva's increasing sensation of writing without a context, and her sense of no longer having an audience. Previously she had envisaged herself as marginal, yet paradoxically central, surrounded by contemporary poets who could be grouped under one 'ism' or another, while she was indefinable. Not only does she have no place in the Soviet society coalescing around her, expressing the political and social views she holds can be dangerous. What results is a hushed, *pianissimo* speech, deliberately hard to understand or decipher, almost a speaking in code, which renders *The Craft*, containing poems composed in the run up to emigration, probably the most challenging of all her volumes for a contemporary reader. 'Roland's Horn' uses the legend of the horn the hero carried, only to be sounded at the moment of greatest desperation (he left it too late) to express Tsvetaeva's resilient, paradoxical conviction that sooner or later, in some time or place, her work will find an understanding audience.

Among the most remarkable items from those months is '"Was he your husband?" – "No"', a dialogue next to a corpse which the first person to speak considers with contempt, while the other – presumably to be more closely identified with the poet – refuses to abandon the imperative of compassion. That is pushed to the very limit when she demands also to be nailed up inside the coffin. 'Eyebrows darting leagues apart' reads as a brief tribute to Tsvetaeva's distant husband, and his loyalty to the counter-revolutionary cause.

The period from spring 1921 till spring 1925 is covered in two chronologically ordered collections in which the uncollected items did not find a place, giving them a rather different status. 1923 was the year, and Prague the setting, for Tsvetaeva's ultimately disastrous relationship with a friend and former comrade in arms of her husband, Konstantin Rozdevich (1895–1988), producing two long poems, *Poem of the Hill* (anyone who has seen the Petřín hill in Prague will know that it cannot be referred to as a mountain) and *Poem of the End*. These have tended to overshadow Tsvetaeva's other work, with the risk of typecasting her as a female poet of unhappy love and little more. 'You who loved me with the lie' must be addressed to Rozdevich, while the Czech capital is portrayed in 'Prague', 'However bitter, gulping down the smoke', 'Pillars in a throne room that's' and 'Eyes'. Ophelia, Ariadne and Phaedra, who all appear in *After Russia*, figure here in 'Along the riverbanks, grey trees show where' and 'Just like into the seas' pure blue'. Pasternak, a constant presence and a constant inspiration for that collection, is addressed in 'Not thundering from passing wheels', while 'Orphaned air beyond the grave' (reminiscent of 'Daybreak on the Railway Lines') expresses Tsvetaeva's near obsession with the railway lines she constantly encountered in travelling between Prague and the village where she resided which, in her imagination, must also somehow or other lead back to Moscow. 'From native villages', another poem about trains, about a journey towards Pasternak, back to Russia and perhaps beyond, is a dazzling technical feat. Tsvetaeva alternates lines of six and ten syllables in rhyming quatrains. In a manner English cannot hope to reproduce, the longer lines end in words accented four syllables from the end, while in the shorter repeated monosyllables evoke the chugging of the locomotive, the obsessively repeated pumping of the pistons which power the train's onward movement. The technical challenges Tsvetaeva sets herself here can seem almost perverse. Read in the original, the poem generates an accumulating sense of wonder and disbelief.

The first eight of Tsvetaeva's *Poems to Blok*, which date from mid-April to mid-May 1916, like the 'Poems to Akhmatova', are included in the first *Milestones*. Like those, they combine homage – whose sincerity is beyond doubt, evident in the way both cycles echo the tone and imagery of the poet in question – and emulation. This cunning literary strategy is both effective and convincing. By paying tribute to those she saw as the most outstanding of her contemporaries (and it is interesting that the poems Mandelstam inspired do not form a cycle of their own), Tsvetaeva demonstrates her generosity towards their achievement while also taking her place among them as their equal. The imagery has a brinkmanship which is at times frightening, as when the sound of Blok's surname is compared to a pistol's trigger cocked at the temple, or when Tsvetaeva's relationship to Akhmatova (whose 'tender singing throttles me,/ a tightening belt') is described as that between a convict and the prison guard accompanying him into exile. A ninth poem, 'Like a faint beam through the pitch dark of Hades', included in *Where Swans Are Camped*, refers to shells exploding not so far away when Tsvetaeva heard Blok read in Moscow, probably at the Polytechnic Museum in early May 1920. The remaining poems (one word is missing in (11)) were composed in August, then November and December 1921. They articulate Tsvetaeva's response to Blok's death, which prompted a letter to Akhmatova that has survived in Tsvetaeva's notebooks. It begins with a meditation on the ultimate unreality of death:

> Death is when I do *not* exist. I cannot perceive my own non-existence. Which means that my death does not exist. Only other people's, i.e., a nearby void, an abandoned place (he's gone but *living* somewhere). His *not-being* doesn't exist, because we are incapable of understanding anything other than subjectively, any different understanding is a parrot-like mimicry of sounds.

There follows a disquieting, indeed, terrifying rejection of embodiment, of the corporeal, which again comes to the fore in *After Russia*:

> Besides which, can my body truly be me? Is *that* what listens to music, writes verses and so on? All the body can do is serve, obey. The body is a garment. What do I care if it gets stolen, which cranny the thief buried it in, under which stone?
> To Hell with it! (Both the garment and the thief.)

The later poems to Blok are haunting and bewildering in their determinedly heterodox deployment of Christian imagery. As before, Blok is seen as a Christlike figure, but one whose resurrection may take the form of reincarnation. In a poem that opens with the arresting image of a roofworker sliding soundlessly off the roof to his death, Tsvetaeva imagines journeying from end to end of Russia in search of the cradle where the newborn poet is concealed. The last poem but one envisages him as Orpheus, unable to resist the impulse to turn and check that Eurydice was indeed following behind, that the divinities of Hades had not tricked him. His severed head now bobs along the surface of the River Hebrus, a scene that recurs in 'Thus did they float, the head, the lyre' from *The Craft*, written five days before the two 'Bethlehem' poems which, Tsvetaeva notes, only by chance failed to find their way into the *Poems to Blok*. Similar images occur in the letter to Akhmatova:

> The amazing thing is not that he died, but that he lived. So few signs of the earthly, so little garment. As if he immediately became the face on an icon, alive and posthumous (in our love). Nothing snapped, nothing got detached. He was such a manifest victory for the spirit, so obviously spirit, that it's amazing life actually – admitted him? (He *so fractured* existence!)
> I perceive Blok's death as a resurrection.
> I gulp back my human pain: for him that's over, we won't think about it (see ourselves in it). I don't want him in the grave, I want him in the dawns. (Extending in that cloud!)

The passage shows Tsvetaeva speculating at the very limits of language, pushing the language to the near point of breakage to see what kind of thoughts are generated there. If in poetry Blok can be angel and Orpheus, crucified Christ and nascent Saviour at one and the same time, poetic illusion was accompanied by a delusion in real life, which provoked the cycle of poems 'His Partner' (an attempt to get closer to the actual meaning of the Russian title than the literal translation 'Girlfriend', 'Woman Friend'). Tsvetaeva believed the rumours according to which the last woman to be in a relationship with Blok, Alexandra Nolle-Kogan (1888–1956), had given birth to his son. Nolle-Kogan is apostrophised as 'Benedicta in mulieribus', the words the angel Gabriel is supposed to have pronounced at the Annunciation. Tsvetaeva deliciously concocts a heretical mixture where both the dying poet and the newborn child become divinities, while the speaker assumes the part of the shepherd girl from 'Bethlehem', first in order precisely because she is the last, the onlooker of least importance. 'With him to the end' is a moving tribute to Nolle-Kogan's unceasing care for Blok on his deathbed. 'Emperors three' foretells an impending catastrophe in the gift brought by the third of the Magi.

Tsvetaeva discussed the matter in her notebooks:

> She showed me his letters – written in a marvellous, powerful, old-fashioned hand – from the times of grandfather (Turgenev) and perhaps also of Pushkin, she showed me his gifts to his son – a rose and a cross, Harlequin, an icon, showed me the son, Sasha, with *his* eyes, *his* eyelashes, *his* forehead, *his* lips (unmistakable). You can see the resemblance, can't you? Showed me a portrait of herself with the son where the artist, unexpectedly, deliberately, making the child a bit older, had him utterly resemble Blok. I'm just back from morning mass, forty days since he died ('Remember, after morning mass/ dear friend, woman of brilliance'), December 1921 to April 29th 1922 (Russian style) (the day we left), inspiring in me an impossible retrospective dream, me as the mother of the son I celebrated at his birth. (Vera Zaitseva's words, 'N.A.K. is expecting Blok's child and is terrified about whether he'll want to be seen at her side when she has such a belly' – when she read my poems to Blok, *he* was inside her!), me bowing down in front of that child like a shepherd in Bethlehem – it all *happened*, I *loved* both her and her son, there was an Annunciation and a Christmas – and I need no immaculate conception, every conception is immaculate, for the blood at giving birth washes it all away – and Blok was an *angel*, so I need no wings...

She then goes on to describe the mockery greeting her gullibility around a café table on Berlin's Prager Diele in spring 1922:

> How is Blok's son?

Blok never had a son.

How can that be, when... I mean, N.A. Kogan's son?

Apparently he's fine. But he was never Blok's son. Blok was unable to have children. And he never had an affair with her.

What about the resemblance then?

You're right, there is a resemblance.

(He names a woman, a poetess apparently, secretary of some St Petersburg writers' or poets' union – could be Gurevich – who saw him, and says it's true, there is a mysterious resemblance.)

Look, my dear, I saw that child, absolutely Blok's features. Think of the photo of Blok as a child! I saw his letters too...

But N. A. makes things up, she's an adventuress, an adorable woman, but we've all known her well for ages, and take my word for it, no one but you believes that legend.

They laugh.

But the letters, written in *his* hand...

N.A. could have forged the letters...

Could she forge Blok's words? 'If it's a son, the one thing I wish him is a conscience?!'

Maybe he too believed it. She may have convinced him. Let me tell you again, Blok could not have children. That's been clearly established now, on a medical basis...

Now he's dead?! Darling, I'm not a doctor, but I simply cannot understand how you can prove something like that posthumously – or when someone's alive. He couldn't, he couldn't, and all of a sudden, he did. All I know is, a son exists, and it's *his* son...

But she was living with two men at the time...

And if there were three? What about the resemblance? Let's accept for a minute that you're right – what need had she of all that *monstrous* playacting? She could have convinced everybody – except herself. And think how *monstrously* lonely – she would have been the only person in the world to know her son wasn't Blok's. How could anyone live with a secret like that? And most of all, why?

You forget Blok left a massive inheritance.

I don't get you. Symbolically? The glory of being Blok's son?

Not a symbol at all, a genuine literary inheritance, the right to publish his books. It all goes to his mother and his wife, but if he had a son...

That's enough now. That's disgraceful. So who are you, Blok's publisher? Maybe it mattered to Blok's *publisher* that there should be no son? The expert once he's died would be a publisher, not a doctor...

Everyone laughs (Helikon, Kaplun, Ehrenburg, the rest of them):

M[arina] I[vanovna]! Why are *you* getting so worked up about it? Whether he's Blok's son, or not Blok's son...

Me (with tears in my eyes) – You're insulting the dead! I saw the letters, I saw the heirloom, the cross – a rose and a cross! – I saw how much she loves that child.

Alkonost: Piotr Semenovich also loves him very much...

Me, with my last breath: I will *never* give in to you...

Alkonost, with a smile: That's regrettable.

Tsvetaeva was never introduced to Blok, who died on August 7th. On August 21st Akhmatova's husband, from whom she had separated, the poet Nikolay Gumilyov, was shot on trumped up charges of conspiracy. Rumours that Akhmatova had committed suicide prompted a further letter from Tsvetaeva on the last day of the month. Lydia Chukovskaya recalled how she saw Akhmatova for the very first time at a memorial evening for Blok, wearing a blue shawl Tsvetaeva had given her.

Tsvetaeva would embark on her own, prolonged march to Calvary via emigration to Prague and then, at the end of October 1925, to Paris. In the 1930s her husband relinquished his commitment to the counter-revolutionary movement and became a Stalinist agent. First their daughter Alya, then Efron himself returned to the Soviet Union. Tsvetaeva and her son followed in June 1939. When she finally met Akhmatova face to face in Moscow, both Alya and Sergei had been arrested. After being evacuated to Yelabuga, Tsvetaeva would take her own life on August 31st 1941.

Budapest
February 2025

MILESTONES 2 (1921)

I

Darkness, and the whole world starts migrating.
Trees wander through the night across the earth,
grapes wander in the form of golden wine,
stars make a pilgrimage from house to house
and rivers, turning, head – back to their source!
While all I want is to – sleep in your arms.

January 14th 1917

No sooner have my burning eyelids closed –
heavenly roses, heavenly rivers.

Somewhere afar,
as if forgotten,
beguiling words from
a serpent in heaven.

Sorrowful Eve,
I recognise the
tree of the Lord
in heaven's circle.

January 20th 1917

Darling fellow travellers we shared a
bivouac with! Miles, more miles, stale bread…
Trundling gypsy wagons, rivers
roaring as they hurried back
where they came from…

Remember gypsy dawns in paradise?
Frantic horses neighing, silvered steppes?
Mountains wreathed in pale blue smoke,
a voice raised in a song about
a gypsy king…

Sheltered by branches ages old, we bore you
sons at black midnight who were just as fair
as night, and just as destitute,
while nightingales kept murmuring
their litanies…

Fellow travellers of those golden days,
our beggars' lovemaking, our beggars' feasts
could not detain you. Bonfires blazed
up high, and our carpets were strewn
with falling stars…

January 29th 1917

Bleary-eyed and menacing
she looked straight at me.
Somewhere a thunderclap replied.
"Now then, young girl,
let's try and see
what awaits you here on earth."

Pale blue cloud banks formed a funnel.
A distant thunderclap – a peal!
The fortune-teller's sleepy eyes
were fixed upon my child.
"What do you foresee?"
"I'll tell the truth."
"Too late for me,
for her too early…"
"Cut the crap, pretty girl! Hear me
out first and then tell me I'm wrong!"
Her filthy hand, with silver rings,
opened a fan of cards.

"Unable to hold your tongue,
straightforward, outspoken,
squandering yourself on life,
you live like a profligate,
a scoundrel will drown you
in a spoonful of water.

"Soon, at night, an unexpected journey…
Not many lines,
luck running out…
Cross my palm with gold!"

A thunder peal – black against black,
the Ace of Spades appears.

May 19th 1917

Kissing the brow – puts care to flight.
I kiss your brow.

Kissing the eyes – ensures sound sleep.
I kiss your eyes.

Kissing the lips – water to drink.
I kiss your lips.

Kissing the brow – forgetfulness.
I kiss your brow.

June 5th 1917

Mud sputters up
under the hooves.
Shawl like a shield
hiding her face.
Matchmakers, have
fun now we're gone!
Carry us off,
dishevelled horse!

Father and mother
holding us back,
now the whole plain's
our marriage bed!
Drunk on no wine, full on no bread.
A gypsy wedding – tearing along!

Top up the glass,
empty again.
Din from guitars, from moon and mud.
Tottering first to the right, then the left.
The gypsy's a prince!
The prince is a gypsy!
Mister, take care – that stuff sure burns!
A gypsy wedding – these are the songs!

Shawls, coats of fur
piled in a heap,
jingling and rustling

of steel, of lips.
Necklaces echo
clinking from spurs.
Somewhere or other,
hand fondling silk.
Howl like a wolf's,
snort like a bull's.
A gypsy wedding – fallen asleep!

June 25th 1917

My spell will conjure you from gold
and from the midnight flying widow,
from the evil fumes of marshes,
from the hag that staggers past,

from snakes that hide beneath a bush,
from water underneath a bridge,
from two roads meeting in a cross,
from woman's fasting and contrition,

from a shawl made in Bukhara,
from an emperor's proclamation,
from black-hearted deeds,
from a snow-white steed!

May 10th 1918

I have a story for you of huge fraud,
a story for you of how mist descends
on young trees and old stumps, a story of
how fires go out in hovels, while a gypsy
migrant from a far-off country blows
into his narrow pipe beneath a tree.

I have a story for you of huge lies,
a story of a slender hand which grasps
a knife, of how a centuries old wind
lifts young men's curls and ruffles old men's beards.

Centuries thundering.
Drumming of hooves.

June 4th 1918

My steed is a consuming fire!
No clattering hooves, no neighing.
Where his breath reached, no spring can gush,
where he passed by, no grass grows.

My steed's a fire – insatiable!
Insatiable fire his rider!
Hair tangled up in his red mane –
a trail of fire – into the skies!

August 14th 1918

Every poem's a child of love,
a beggar child, a bastard.
Firstborn exposed in the gutter,
a tribute paid to the four winds.

Hell and altar to the heart,
paradise and infamy.
And its father? Who's to say?
An emperor, a robber.

August 14th 1918

I'm giving you this comb so you'll remember
me longer than an hour, lad, or a year.

The reason little gold combs got invented
was so young lovers won't forget their girls.

So the one I love won't drink without me –
comb, little comb for straightening my hair!

This one is special, there's no other like it –
pulled through my hair, its teeth feel just like strings!

The moment that you touch it, all the chatter
is about me, nobody else comes up.

So the one I love won't sleep without me –
comb, little comb for straightening my hair!

So that every inch he puts between us
can seem to him a mile of burning sweat,

each mile as he returns seem like an inch –
that's why little gold combs got invented.

So the one I love can't live without me –
seven strings that straighten out my hair!

November 2nd 1918

Into this drink I have dissolved
a fistful of burnt hair for you
to stop you eating, stop you singing,
stop you drinking, stop you sleeping,

to make sure your youth is joyless,
so your sugar won't be sweet,
so when darkness falls no young
woman cuddles in your arms.

Just as these gold curls of mine
were transformed to ashen grey,
so may your years as a young man
become cold and white as winter.

So you'll go blind and deaf,
dry out, a clump of moss,
vanish, a sigh.

November 3rd 1918

But on my forehead stars
– take note! – are burning.
In my small right hand – heaven,
in my small left hand – hell.

The silken belt I carry
wards off all afflictions.
My head reposes on
the book of Kingly Realms.

Many are like me
here in holy Russia –
you should ask the winds,
you should ask the wolves.

From one land to the next,
one city to the next,
in my small right hand – heaven,
in my small left hand – hell.

I gave you heaven mixed with hell to drink,
now your whole life is like one single day.

See me on my way,
bridegroom, for seven leagues!
Many are like me
here in holy Russia.

July 1919

My way does not lead past your house.
My way leads past nobody's house.

And yet I keep going astray
(especially in spring),
I keep yearning for people, like
a dog beneath the moon.

Welcome in everybody's home,
I let nobody sleep!
Play dominoes with grandad, sing
songs with his grandson.

I don't make women jealous – I'm
merely a voice, a glance.
I never had a lover build
a mansion just for me.

Merchants, your riches mean nothing
to me, they make me laugh!
I build palaces, bridges of
my own within one night.

(Pay no attention to my words!
They're women's babbling!)
When morning dawns, with my own hands
I tear down what I built.

Like a straw sheaf, the mansion's gone!
My way does not lead past your house.

May 14th 1920

My bearing's unpretentious,
my home has a low roof.
The archipelago
I come from's far away!

I don't need anyone!
He entered – sleepless nights.
I'd set my house on fire
to warm a stranger's meal.

One look – he was a friend.
He entered – he can stay.
Our laws could not be simpler:
written in our blood.

I lure the darling moon
down onto my palm.
He's gone – he might have never
been, the same for me.

I look at the knife's mark:
will it have time to heal
before the first newcomer
asks me for a drink?

August 1920

Hunchbacks, beggars, thieves – I've kissed them all!
Larking around with convicts – mere child's play!
My scarlet lips weren't made for saying no,
come forward, leper – I won't turn you down!

As long as I'm young –
water to a goose!
Never tell anyone:
No!
Always: Yes!

What does it matter you're ragged and shoeless:
I'm as indifferent as death with his scythe!
What if they say you're a gypsy, a horse thief?
And there's still more that they say about you…

Who cares you're penniless –
hoof fits the foot!
Never tell anyone:
No!
Always: Yes!

Flashing, dancing, whiplashes – red paint!
But I won't kiss my executioner!

Moscow, November 1920

II

And God said:
Young flesh,
Arise!

And the flesh sighed:
– God, just let me
sleep.

Jaira's daughter
just wants peace.

And God said:
Sleep.

March 1917

All you need do is live! – I let my hands
fall, let my burning forehead rest on them.
That's how a youthful Storm hearkens to God
out of doors, at some dark hour of night.

And all at once a mighty palm was laid,
as from the sky, on my breath's towering wave,
someone or other's lips pressed against mine.
That's how God hearkens to a youthful Storm.

June 20th 1917

I stand with head thrown back and lowered eyes
before the face of God and all his saints
on this my festival, my Judgement Day.

In the young angels' ranks confusion, tears.
The righteous are impassive. From your throne
of clouds, only you gaze down like a friend.

Ask me anything you want to. Old,
and good, you know I cannot lie with such
tolling from the Kremlin's bells inside me.

You know how passionately Providence
and Waywardness battled both day and night
in the turning millstone of my ribs.

And so, a mortal woman, eyes downcast,
but forehead lifted like an angry angel's,
I stand before you at the Emperor's gate
- look! – on the day of the Annunciation.

But, dove departing from my breast, my voice
describes a circle in the crimson dome.

March 1918

Flesh for the flesh, for the spirit, spirit,
bread for the flesh, for the spirit, news,
worms for the flesh, for the spirit sighs,
seven garlands, seven firmaments.

Mourn, flesh! Tomorrow you'll be dust!
No tears, spirit! Be glorified!
Slavery today, tomorrow
ruling all seven firmaments.

May 9th 1918

I'm no impostor, I've made my way home.
I'm no maidservant, I've no need of bread.
I'm your passion and your Sunday rest,
your week's seventh day, your seventh heaven.

There on earth they would give me a farthing,
and kept hanging millstones around my neck.
How could you fail to recognise me, my
beloved? Your dear swallow – Psyche, me!

April 1918

My darling, you are clothed in rags
which at one time were tender flesh.
I tore it, wore it all away
and now only two wings are left.

Clothe me in your magnificence,
have mercy on me, rescue me.
As for these poor, decayed tatters,
store them where the vestments are.

May 13th 1918

Words are traced out in the nighttime sky –
eyes immensely beautiful go blind…
Dying is no longer fearsome,
making love no longer sweet.

Writing in sweat, tilling in sweat!
A different ardour's known to us:
a light fire dancing on my curls,
inspiration breathed into me!

May 14th 1918

I bless the labour of each day,
I bless the sleep of every night,
God's mercy and his judgement too,
his law, gentle, or hard as stone,

my dusty mantle, purple, tattered,
my dusty stick, so filled with rays…
And then, Lord, peace in a strange house,
bread in an oven not my own.

May 21st 1918

Tears, tears – stream of living water!
Tears, tears – blessèd calamity!
Welling up from burning entrails,
flowing out from burning eyes.
God's anger is broad and abundant
yet somehow people cope with it.

For once draw from these lips
a sigh that isn't stale.
Knock on my ribcage
using your staff of light!

May 1918

Hands useless to the one we love
can be of use serving the World.
The lyre has crowned us with a grievous
title: "Woman of the World".

Few are invited to the emperor's
feast – the rest must sing for supper!
The World, not the beloved, is
eternal – we don't serve in vain.

July 6th 1918

Our two souls are as near
as the right and left hands.

We're close, contented, warm
just like a pair of wings.

But then a gale gets up –
a chasm gapes between!

July 10th 1918

Knight resembling an angel, Duty!
Heaven's sentinel!
White as a gravestone set upon
these living ribs of mine.

Behind the wings upon my shoulders,
keyholder, you emerge,
my watchman throughout every night,
bell-ringer every morning.

Passion, youthfulness and pride
gave in without resisting,
because you were the first to swear
obedience to this slave!

July 14th 1918

Courage, virginity – a combination
ancient and wonderful as death and glory.
I swear it by the red blood flowing through
my veins, and by the curls upon my head –

this back of mine will bear no other burden
than the blessed burden of the World!
I place my gentle hand upon the sword,
upon the white swan's neck that is my lyre.

July 27th 1918

So, tossing my head back –
youthful Russia, give ear! –
I refute these foul calumnies
on Beauty and the Soul.

Over pubs filled with sin, small change,
blood, tatters, broken faith –
oh my soul's Trinity, arise!
Lily – Swan – and the Lyre.

July 1918

Bring me what everyone else has no need for:
all of it has to burn down on my fire!
I make no distinction between life and death,
beckoning both, weightless gifts to my fire.

Flames are delighted with things that are weightless:
undergrowth, garlands and words from last year…
Similar nourishment makes them dart upwards!
You, too must resurrect, purer than ash!

Since I'm a phoenix, if I'm going to sing
fire must surround me – hold my life aloft!
I burn up on high, I burn right to the end,
so as to light up the night that is yours.

Ice-cold conflagration, a fountain of fire!
My stature's immense and I carry it high,
carry on high the high office I hold –
Partner in Dialogue, Inheritress!

September 2nd 1918

It's my pleasure to offer an example
by living simply, like a pendulum,
the sun, the calendar, a lay hermit,
slimly built and wise like all God's creatures.

To know the Spirit leads me, fights beside me,
to enter unannounced – a ray, a glance –
to live as I write, succinct, an example,
as God commanded, and my friends do not.

November 22nd 1918

If stanzas cannot help, nor constellations,
then this must be what's known as retribution
because, time and again,

straightening up over an awkward line,
above my spacious forehead I would look
for stars only, not eyes;

because, acknowledging your suzerainty,
not for one single moment, gorgeous Eros,
did I regret your absence

when, in night's ritual obscurities,
from a crimson, yielding mouth I looked
for rhymes only, not lips;

because, however harshly judged, as white
as snow beneath this left breast, I became
eternally a god!

And, face to face with the young Orient,
because I looked upon my lofty forehead
not for roses, but dawns!

May 20th 1920

Love! Love! Convulsed by spasms, in the grave
on the alert, still tempted, confused, darting –
my darling! Whether snow, or clouds are piled
upon my tomb, I won't bid you farewell.

I wasn't given two exquisite wings
so hundredweights could press upon my heart.
I won't get added to the wretched horde
swaddled in shrouds that neither see nor speak.

Working my hands loose, I shall wriggle free
and break out from your clutches, death, with one
rapid manoeuvre! For a thousand leagues
around the snow will melt, the forests burn!

And if, clenching them all – wings, shoulders, knees –
I let them carry me to the churchyard,
it will be only to mock putrefaction,
rise as a verse, or blossom as a rose!

around November 28th 1920

I know I will die at the edge of the day – but at which
I have no way of saying. It can't be laid on to request.
If only the flame of my torch could be extinguished twice!
Simultaneously when darkness falls, and new day fills the sky!

I walked on the earth to the steps of a dance, Heaven's daughter,
in a pinafore crammed full of roses, and damaged no bud!
I know I will die at the edge of the day. God would never
send falcon-black night to collect my soul, white as a swan's!

Gently pushing aside a cross I'll have refused to kiss,
I'll soar into the unbounded sky to receive my farewell
with the answering rift of a smile at the point where it parts…
I'll still be a poet when struggling to catch my last breath!

Moscow, December 1920

UNCOLLECTED POEMS 1920–1925

LYRICS FROM THE DRAMA "THE DISCIPLE"

1

When rolling waves
break on the pale
blue sea, it turns to grey.

When love comes to
a heart that's young
it learns what "faithful" means.

God, when rollers break, protect
my boat, my wretched home!
And protect from evil love
the heart that is my home!

2

'Faithful', she says,
adds 'very'. Next day –
'You're not the dancer for me!'
I won't grow into such a flower –
better, head beneath the axe!

Let the red-shirted forester
separate crown from trunk –
his mother won't need to regret
she didn't spend that night alone.

I didn't dream this wondrous horror –
marriage before a king!
An axe can act as my bridegroom,
the scaffold be my altar!

3

I came to you in search of bread,
the holy bread of every day.
Like entering heaven itself
more than beneath a roof!

Only God on his starry throne
can feed so generously!
May the good shepherd find, dear God,
shelter beneath your palm!

Hoisting my sail, I won't forget
your welcoming bread and salt!
Three misfortunes in the world:
hunger, passion, old age…

He spared me one, as for the other –
it's a long way away!
And I left not a thing behind
with the blue-eyed girl!

Poets, we're like sailors: never
too early to lift anchor!
There are three freedoms in the world:
songs, bread and the sea…

4

There, along a rope drawn taut
midst papier-mâché cliffs,
did you, while you were sleepwalking,
take the skies by storm?

Ruler of new realms, son of
unearthly latitudes –
as if your skin was being flayed –
that is how you smiled.

A deafening beating of drums.
Nobles and paupers rushed
so their crazy lips could close
that living wound of yours.

I recall a parched, uncanny
smile that failing strength inspired!
Only then it looked as though
you were wearing a skirt …

5

(Sailors and Poets)

Midst wild sailors and simple fishermen
for jesters and for poets
a table always waits.

The sea can be our bread,
the sea can be our salt,
the sea can be our glass,
the sea can be our wine.

Sailors and poets – fledglings of one mother,
no-one's sons, no-
body's fathers.

We are a joyous guild!
The sea's where we're baptised!
The sea is our see-saw!
The sea's our carousel!

Girls turning up will always be made welcome –
the only risk with us
is stitches coming loose!

White foam can be our bed,
white foam can be our mattress,
white foam can be our pillow,
white foam beneath our heads.

6

(The Singer – to the Girls)

Girls looking to enjoy yourselves
– I can't remember all your names –
girls looking to enjoy yourselves,
the singer sends his deepest bow.

Welcome me, prodigal son,
into the flock of outcast sheep:
it makes no difference in God's eyes
if you're a whore – or else a poet.

For a pretzel on Twelfth Night
we relinquished our good name:
some of us for money, some
sold ourselves for a soul.

Stoking up Gehenna's blaze,
Devil, please don't scrounge the wood!
Without blinking an eyelid, in
the singer goes, takes the whore's place.

Even if stripped of our honour,
even with a murky conscience,
iron can bleach us in a trice,
burning white hot, make us white!

No mess table, a throne room –
we're confronting God the Father! –
getting down upon his knees
before a whore – it's me, the singer!

7

Dancing round, dancing round,
why the beating feet?
Roam the seas, roam the seas,
why sail so far off?

Dancing on a burning floor, I'm
frightened I'll get scorched.
Want to know why I don't cry?
I'm laughing far too much!

Sailor guy, our sailor guy,
sailor on the sea!
Sadness is merely a worm,
small and wriggling.

He went to make his fortune, came
back with a string of beads.
Want to know why I don't cry?
I'm laughing far too much!

The oceans are ever so deep!
Roll over one more time!
Such a waste, a handsome guy
flung out for fish to eat!

God's generous, I waste it all!
My whole load – a bronze cross.
Want to know why I don't cry?
I'm laughing far too much!

between May 25th and July 13th 1920

8

Parting's your trade. Why should you care
about a bonfire cooling down?
One wave arriving rolled you in,
another took you off.

Why should I, carried in
no mother's womb, but in the sea's,
crawl around, a furious slave,
searching for the man I love?

As if it was an apple, darling
friend, bite into the whole globe!
Chatting to the ocean depths,
it's still me you'll be chatting to!

She won't take it lying down
like a girl who's born on land –
a daughter carried in no mother's
womb, but in the sea's!

No, *our* girls shed no tears, they don't
write letters, wait for news!
I'll just set off to fish again –
no net, no weights, no floats!

Whatever power my song may have's
a mystery to me –
I who was carried in no mother's
womb, but in the sea's!

And my estate – I've given all
my life, but not for free!
Treading pebbles by the shore
it's my own ribs I'm treading on!

Like a captured queen on trial,
all I can testify –
I was carried in no mother's
womb, but in the sea's!

June 13th 1920

9

Last night you gazed into my eyes –
now you won't even look at me!
You'd sit with me till dawn birds sang –
now all the skylarks became crows!

I'm stupid, you're the clever one,
alive, and I'm a frozen pillar.
Women's wail down the centuries:
'Darling, what was it I did wrong?'

Her tears are water, her blood too –
she washed myself in tears and blood!
No mother, a stepmother – Love:
don't look for justice, or for mercy.

Ships carry our loved ones away,
a white road takes them far from us...
A moan resounding through the world:
'Darling, what was it I did wrong?'

Yesterday you lay at my feet!
Compared me to the Chinese Empire!
Then suddenly unclasped your hands,
let life fall, like a rusty coin!

On trial for murdering a child,
unprepossessing and fainthearted,
even in Hell I'll say to you:
'Darling, what was it I did wrong?'

I ask the table, ask my bed:
'Why do I suffer so much pain?'
'Tired of you, he's kissing someone
else now – that's what tortures you'.

You showed me life in the fire's heart,
then cast me out on frozen steppes.
Darling, look what *you* did to me!
Where was the wrong that *I* did you?

I know it all – don't contradict!
Love's over, I see clearly now!
Where Love's no longer to be found,
Death the Reaper takes its place.

What point shaking an apple tree?
The ripe fruit falls when its time comes.
Pardon me, love, for everything,
for all the wrong that I did you!

June 14th 1920

TO THE JEWS

Disinterested, indifferent to silver,
a teenage tenderness, the air's pale blue,
I welcome you today and in the future
until time ends. Amen.

I cancel what a twofold enmity
wrote in my blood – the daughter of a priest
and of a Polish noblewoman. Welcome
to the Kremlin, strange and marvellous spring!

Blackened, betrayed, vanquished, sold – the Kremlin!
Carrion crows circle above its domes.
Like ordinary people I, too, used
the word "yid", making the sign of the cross.

Fratricide intoxicated me, the
Orthodox cross cast God into shadow!
But as for him – there was no point in changing
his name, putting Heinrich in place of Harry!

You sang of grenadiers in Russian fields,
you were the shadow that Napoleon's wing
cast, and to me you won't stop being a "yid"
until the domes are gleaming bright once more!

May 1920

Roses will blossom tomorrow
where I let tears fall today.
I've been embroidering fine lace,
tomorrow I'll be weaving nets.

For me, all of the sky can take
the sea's place, and all of the earth.
My net of poetry's much more
than a straightforward fishing net!

June 15th 1920

EARTHLY NAME

A glass of water when thirst parches you –
'Give me one! Or I'll die!'
Not giving up, flagging, melodious
(complaint in burning heat)

I keep repeating, still more savagely
again and yet again –
like when it's dark, you only want to sleep
but you're not able to.

As though meadows lacked sleep-inducing herbs
for all anxieties!
Persistently – repeated pointlessly –
a child's first syllable…

With every moment more and more unique,
strap tightening round the neck…
If all that's to be had here is an earthly
name, that's not what counts.

between 16th and 25th June 1920

Sunset's darling blaze was ended,
the soldiers marched off in a line.
My mother told me on her deathbed:
Dress up just like you were a boy.

The whole white road going past our house
is at those young lads' beck and call.
However light-footed, no girl
can find her way to distant hearts!

My mother mused, the soldiers sang –
right up until she breathed her last
the foot of the bed never stopped
shaking – for she'd been a dancer!

…If a breaking heart undoes
the stitches when no doctor's near,
know there's a head for every heart
and, for every head, an axe…

June 1920

Though still alive, I fold my arms.
I'll die without taking communion.
A fissure cuts right through my soul.
My case is well and truly lost.

As for you, you'd like to know
what I'm being punished for –
look beyond the window: there
you'll find my case clearly set out.

June 1920

Denying God, the Wandering Jew
angered him, and so was punished.
Seeing how we all are punished,
denying God, refusing to
deny his creatures – where's the difference?

June 1920

A home at whose door no one knocks:
poor people have nothing to guard.
A home where no one's ill at ease:
feel free to sit down, or stretch out.

The only rule is, never judge
<...>
It was love shattered the windows,
and the wind tore off the roof.

A filled glass awaits everyone –
<...> even you, Cain!
You're the householder, just like me
and I'm a guest, as much as you.

What is given without payment –
that's my way of getting rich!
A fire shattered the windows, winter
took the door from off its hinges!

Unsugared tea and wholemeal bread –
but my face is white instead!
I share with everybody what
was left, the things they didn't take.

Hard undoing my apron strings?
We've got a serving maid – she'll help!
Feel free to dance, but watch your step.
Bowing deep has holed the floor!

You want to dance, or to stretch out?
No one will raise objections here.
The boots you're wearing are too tight?
What are these hands of mine for then?

And if she gave you too much love –
spit in her eye – she's got a sleeve!
The only rule is, never judge.
The only edict, no-one pays.

June 28th 1920

Just equals, same as yes and no,
like a black flower, and a white
or, in creation's thundering hour,
two masses – Kremlin, Caucasus.

Earthly measures mean nothing here.
The summits' children are all equals.

Competing in baseness – leave that
for worms and for the mob to do.
In the thundering hour of grace,
all mountains are each other's brothers!

Thus, in defiance of all laws,
our two hands grasped each other.

========

Given you have a yellow eye,
you're eagle, gypsy, wolf to me.

The gypsy stuffed me in a bag,
from painful drudgery the eagle
swept me off to a mountain cliff.

– The wolf lies, tame, next to my feet.

<June–July 1920>

If I give somebody my hand
it's to tell fortunes, not to kiss.

Can you tell me, passer-by,
following pale blue roads of rivers

which is the sea I'll come upon?
Which is the tumbler where I'll drown?

'The wave able to throw you on
your back has yet to lift its crest.

For you all tumblers will be empty,
yourself an ocean to the lips.

Knock tumbler after tumbler back,
drown all of us, you deep blue sea!'

============

And if I take somebody's hand
it's not to tell fortunes, but kiss.

Spider, I got myself entangled
in a web my own hands made.

I'm not going to lift my forehead –
what's the fate I bring to you?

<*July 1920*>

'How many men do you keep up with?
Enough to fill a court, no doubt?'
Even without the odds and ends,
forgive me, I couldn't keep count.

'How many got the whole way there?
Enough to fill a market place?'
Using the tassels on my shawl,
forgive me, I couldn't keep count.

'If you set their hearts end to end,
tell me, would you get to China?'
Typhus has me in its grasp, friend!
If I die, I'll count them up.

========

Two hands, five quick-moving
fingers on each one.
Each of them has a ring
(some of them have two).

Two hands, all the fingers,
add to them the rings –
you wouldn't reach a fifth
<of the> lovers I've had!

<June to July 1920>

Love, honour – I don't give a damn.
– They make your head spin! – Not for me.
That apple on the hawker's tray,
small and enticing – no attraction!

A sort of chain is tugging at my heels,
it can't be long till thunder starts to peal.

What I'd love –
what I'd love –
to die without a sound!

<July 1920>

Wind, oh wind that sweeps along,
sweeps the traces away!
Flying like a red bird into
foreheads of white stone.

Diving, a long-legged dog,
along fields sown with oats.
– Wind, oh wind, losing the place
for an embroidered skirt!

Plague-bearing, coloured indigo,
announcing mutiny –
empty-headed gallows bird,
I grip you in my fist!

Enough of clowning on steep slopes,
battering heads with snow –
knotting the two ends of my scarf
I've bound you hand and foot!

I'm settling accounts with you
for all your jailbird acts –
wearing a leather jerkin, wind –
a red star on your brow!

July 1920

I picture you with dark eyes – separation!
Separation! – tall and set apart.
A smile that flashes like a pocket knife.
Nothing in you like me – separation!

Like all mothers who died prematurely –
separation! – including my own.
Checking your veil in the hall – Anna bent
over a sleeping Sergei – separation!

Straying into a home, jaundice-eyed gypsy –
separation! – a Moldavian woman!
Not knocking on the door, plague-ridden whirlwind
taking our veins by storm – just like a fever!

Searing, chiming, stamping, whistling, roaring,
thundering – like torn silk, or a grey wolf,
sparing neither grandfather nor grandson,
eagle owl, a filly on the steppes!

Razin's kin – broad-shouldered, ginger-haired,
raging – did I see you stirring up a pogrom,
disembowelling guts and feather beds,
separation?

==============

        Now your name's – Marina!

end of July 1920

Others with eyes and with a brilliant face –
night after night I converse with the wind.
Not with a young Zephyr
from Italy –
a Russian crosswind,
splendid and wide-ranging!

Others – all flesh – lose their way amidst flesh,
gulp down the breath of lips that have grown dry –
I throw my arms wide – frozen stiff – lockjaw!
A Russian crosswind can snuff out my soul!

Others – the fetters binding them are sweet!
Aeolus, however, treats us harshly.
Don't worry, you won't thaw! We're of a kind!
As if I weren't a woman at all!

August 2nd 1920

Disappearing into the black night,
tossing aside your cloak, as long ago
Joseph did. I look at its black gleam,
the earth's \<in flames\> – and the heart wants to die.

This year July was pitiless, an acrid
smell of burning forests fills the air,
fumes in my ears, two steps further more fumes,
above Moscow the sun's a bleeding eye.

Burning from peaty swamps. – My mouth is parched.
Rain doesn't want to fall on so much sin!
I'm looking at your cloak – a brilliant splash!
You won't come back to get it in a hurry.

\<beginning of August 1920\>

June, July – time of warbling nightingales.
There was something birdlike in each of us
if, troubling the nightingale-filled night
each on our own account, we two expired!

August's an emperor. Doesn't like roulades.
He'd rather have October cannonades.
August's an emperor. You've no need of one.
Without an emperor, I've no need of you!

\<August 1920\>

<...> if there's nothing to be done!
Surely it's better – pistol to the temple?
For three evenings, three whole evenings long
I yearned for you till I could yearn no more.

I waited for you at the windowsill
more eagerly than foe awaiting foe.
Treading lightly, love, you must tread lightly!
Baseness has no problems moving fast!

Keep your eyes peeled, so the thief of love
doesn't escape along a different path.
Insomniac soul of mine, always on guard,
when I was young you learned how not to sleep!

The dove is heartless. Well, I'll enter this
into the little book of Separations:
I didn't yearn for you, I fished you out
with all the force of hands that were no woman's!

Only to wake bereft the following morning
everything spick and span <...>
I didn't yearn for you or pull you out –
I threw you out of me, push after push!

August 8th 1920

Down in the basements, windows decked in red,
a wretched wailing from accordions –
you'd think none of all this ever occurred –
flags, sacks and bayonets, the Bolsheviks.

Russia's soul got so blended with the basements
you'd think none of all this ever occurred –
you'd think they'd never dug graves on Red Square,
so many coats of arms not been left headless.

<...> palm clutching palm –
our life so merged with the accordions
you'd think the Internationale had not
been our guest here for as long as a day.

August 1920

(fragment)

Like people drinking in deep gulps –
no time to catch their breath –
remembering, forgetful, eyes
shut, I delight in you!

Like golden liquid surging down
the throat, gulp upon gulp,
remembering each syllable,
I gulp your Gallic speech!

August 1920

It all over again: once more a shy
hand presses on the bell.
(Who could compare my living quarters to
a casket, satin-lined?)

It all over again: arms flung wide like
some Polish nobleman.
(But it's not bad getting a change from Kazan
boots, a gypsy's arms!)

It all over again: eyebrows, eyelashes,
and silk so suits her face.
(It does no harm, friend, after coarser fabrics –
the talk, that doesn't change!)

It all over again: <...>
<...>
(After lofty words and crew-cuts, chirping,
hair tied back in a bun!)

It all over again: the emperor's statues
had guards of honour too.
(I won't exhaust you – something I learned from
girls begging on the streets!)

It all over again: down on his knees,
then steel deflecting me.
(I think about your beastly laziness –
pity you like a beast!)

It all over again: <...>
At the door: Please come back!
(Splendid changeover: no more Sèvres porcelain,
a soldier's tin saucepan.)

It all over again: not our own masters,
for ivy needs an oak.
(Swapping my hay bag for a silken alcove –
I can only applaud!)

It all over again: too many harness
buckles, and jingling spurs <...>
(I can sin in different ways, not this one:
no spurs, and no <...>!)

Once more: one hand holds me, the other holds
a cigarette stub. (He
smokes like a Turk, not opening his eyes!
Now who'd put up with that?)

Again: the bedsheets burning hot, he tries
his hardest not to yawn.
(The man yawns, but the woman can't stop crying.
Some Paradise, alcove!)

Again: asleep, his little bird forgotten,
child in a field of rye...
(All that I ask – don't get into the habit
of calling me Marina!)

1920

Hear your willing servant, God,
stifling for one hundred years
because my blood gives me no peace.

A hundred years without deciding
which city I should take, which gates
to tear apart using my hands.

They lead you off to stroll through gardens –
nobody here can use a knife,
nobody takes pity on me.

No peace from the rich blood that pumps
in my ears like a tocsin bell,
a hammer beating at my temples,

clouding my eyes, covered in crimson,
the blood, so ample in its power,
of a captive "bogatyr".

Falling in time, like a pine-cone
or prematurely shoved into
a pond by urchins – not for me!

Sipping acid when you call me –
I wouldn't dare – the noose, a lolling
tongue – the notion makes me sick!

If it's my advice you want –
have me tear down some city's gates
in one go, and then storm the place –

I've done enough asking for things!
Deal me an honourable wound
for Russia, for my country's sake!

August 30th 1920

Feats get accomplished. Poems on those death-
bed scenes don't travel round the villages.
No room for them in saints' lives, and no space
for them to breathe on iconostases.

I put my blood under such strain that seven
binding seals could not hold it more tightly.
Pulling her skull-cap down with a clenched fist,
that's how Empress Sophia blocked her tears!

<1920>

THE WOLF

What had been friendship turned to service,
so then, farewell, my brother wolf!
Our friendship's given up the ghost,
now I'm your duty, not a gift!

Put some leagues between us, then
add a few more on top of those!
I caressed your furry back
while you were consumed with longing!

I won't have you committing crimes,
no sin of mine will leave you guilty,
my insatiability
can keep everyone well fed!

Rather than hunt you through the forests
with flint and fire, as God ordained,
the main thing women want to do
is make sure that your paws stay warm.

I'll lift no finger to detain you,
a finger's not a staff, the woods
are big. Then off with your grey fur,
farewell to you, my brother fang!

Farewell to you, grey hide! And don't
recall me, even in your dreams!
You'll find another female fool
to put her trust in a wolf's grey.

October 1920

Don't tell anyone my name –
I'm your seraph, easily borne –
kiss the top of my head softly
and then leave me to the darkness.

We sat up all night in the dark.
You will forget what made me, me.

Don't let it trouble you – dear God! –
this sigh that briefly sets a garment
fluttering. Could this song blossom,
Friend, upon the lips of lovers?

Go in peace, as though you had
caressed a boy in the church choir.

Spirits, children? Unimportant!
Lad, no one answers for souls!
Would these hands strangle with a rope?
And this tenderness – does it burn?

Remember how, hands at my sides
and petrified, I gazed at you.

In your house I won't be a guest,
I'll let my youthful conscience slacken.
Preparing for great battles, watch me
walk off alone into the dark.

And promise that no golden bird
will beat its wings against your window!

November 25th 1920

TO AN ALIEN

We follow different flags. No place
where these two heads can meet.
Fallen into a snake's clutches,
my soul remains a dove's.

I won't rush round the tree of May
amidst the dancing Reds.
Far loftier than all earthly gates
are Heaven's gates to me.

Your victories mean nothing to me!
I dreamed of different ones.
Not opposite ends of Earth for us
but different galaxies!

Enthusiasts for two different stars –
what am I then to do,
who demolish bridges with
this daring hand of mine?

I possess a hoard that's still
more precious than my icons.
Listen: a different law exists,
above all other laws.

Before it every blade is lowered,
every sapphire grows dim –
the law of an extended hand,
a spirit open wide.

Know that a single measure will
be used to judge us two.
The Heaven in which I believe
is one we both shall see.

Moscow, November 28th 1920

I know that velvet-like fragility –
sturdier than armour! – rounded, chilly shoulders,
two extended creases thinness caused
along the velvet of

your ribs, which I'll not press myself against –
how tender to the cheek! – for there's the rub,
the hurt in it, just velvet to the cheek,
not soul against your chest!

I know, too, how your forehead looks caught in
unswervingly just palms, as if resting
on cypress wood – more easily to shift
over to my own palms,

although it's never going to find its way
to where they lie, indifferent and immense,
spread open like the pages of a book,
stiffening on my knees.

December 2nd 1920

"Farewell!" – Splashing across the countryside,
those syllables: "Farewell!"
A tremor of alarm, parching the lips!
The entire firmament begins to shake!
"Farewell!" – Into that single word
I tip out all my soul!

December 8th 1920

Hair like brief wings, a flurry
amidst the stars – I remember
hair like brief wings beneath
a dust of stars,
lips effort twisted –
burned! –
and every tendon of
those arms.

Lowered eyelids, a
black brightness peeping
through.
Not smoothing, cutting into
a vulnerable, tender
wooden plank – so as to
leap higher, still higher,
the executioner
deaf to rattling,
crunching bones.
Stop!
Too much for the sinews!
A talon
cuts into living flesh!
God help me!

A Paganini "étude" on
one string.

December 1920

'Was he your husband?' 'No.'
'Do you believe souls resurrect?' 'I don't.'
'Then why bow, beat your breast?'
Leaving,
a punch delivered to the heart:
'Poor thing, does he suddenly feel
scared, being so alone?'

'Don't get it!
Was he your husband?' 'No.'
'Do you believe souls resurrect?' 'I don't.'
'So, mouldy, rotten?'
'Mouldy, rotten, yes.'
'Then spit!
Plenty more live souls in the marketplace!'
'Won't he get cold,
no mattress? Lying on bare boards
just like a banished convict?
So hard!'

'The devil take him!
He's dead!
Touch the hollow of his eye:
he doesn't blink!
A hound! He stinks!'
'Don't be so harsh.
His temple, look,
the sweat's not dry yet.
A letter might still bring him greetings,
someone sew him a shirt…'

'Was he your husband?' 'No.'
'Do you believe souls resurrect?' 'I don't.'
'So, end of story!' '…knit him
a smock… I'm going to lie down next to him..
Now then! The nails!'

December 1920

THE BOLSHEVIK

Lake Ilmen to the Caspian Sea –
your shoulders are as broad as that.
The crimson blush of ancient Russian
warriors beats in your cheeks.

Trembling – all across your massive
head – forests rise up. And yet
once an axe is in your hands,
the forest is reduced to splinters!

Two conflagrations: eyes and cheeks.
My God, his blood has to be good!
See how he stands, hands on his haunches,
there in the middle of the yard!

He'd wreck the entire world – armholes
too tight, no room for him to breathe!
I laugh, entrust myself to his
expansive goodness – like a thief's!

Checking new territory out –
So what's the virgin soil like, then?
I laugh – top to toe holy Russia,
blood the colour of raspberries!

January 31st 1921

ROLAND'S HORN

A darling jester tells tales of his grim
deformity, I of my orphanhood…

Behind the prince, his clan, a host behind
the seraph, for each thousands just like him –

stumbling, he falls against a living wall
and knows thousands are there to take his place!

His regiment's a soldier's pride, his legion
a devil's, thieves have riff-raff, jesters humps.

Finally tired of having only conscience
to guide me, fighting as my destiny

while idiots hoot, Philistines laugh out loud –
standing alone – for all – opposed to all! –

swooping high, petrified, I send this thundering
call into the empty wastes of air.

The fire burning inside me is a pledge
some Charlemagne will hear your summons, horn!

March 1921

Away the path tears,
straight to the ether.
– Stop! – Youth, unseeing,
wants to soar higher,
higher still into
the pale blue of rye!
– Stop! – And your next step
takes you to heaven.

August 25th 1921

Competition's scab did not
preside over our births.
Our division was simple – you
Petersburg, Moscow me.

Blessèd and disinterested,
my daïmon observed yours.
At each sigh of your pen, in me
breath lifted like a wave –

how it fell, my proud Polish wave!
From hills in golden dawns
my volunteers arrived, and formed
a crowd around your tent.

Will my poetic adulation
reach the ether's void?
I'm inconsolable, bearing
the woman's lyre alone.

September 12th 1921

Pride, shyness – daughters of one mother
hovered, friends, above my cradle.

'Keep your head high!' pride commanded.
'Cast your eyes down!' shyness whispered.

So I proceed – with downcast eyes,
head held up high – Shyness and Pride.

September 20th 1921

Not for these flattering vestments, lying cassocks
was I born in the world with such a voice!

My dreams don't come at night, but eyes wide open!
I'm not alive like you – whispers and hisses –

in my case whispers, hisses turned into
a lyre, but one whose curve was like a swan's!

My union is with laurels, dawns and winds
I don't live like a monk – I live it up!

As for a guy – fair-haired and not bad-looking! –
well, it failed to work out all too often –

in my case whispers, hisses turned into
a lyre, but one whose curve was like a swan's!

People say a woman's lot is heavy!
I never weighed it – how am I to tell?

My wares are not for sale, they go for free!
That's how you get blue stains under your nails –

in my case screeching, wheezing turned into
a lyre, but one whose curve was like a swan's!

December 4th 1921

HIS PARTNER

> *'Ave' not falling silent,*
> *Eastertide Mass...*
> *Highest of praise*
> *for the last of his women.*

(1)

He sleeps, the joy your torment brought,
he sleeps, heart's heaven won through pain.
You who are blessèd, let me pause
above the Georgian Virgin's cradle.

Neither vanity nor envy
brought me here – don't turn me out!
I've come to praise your little boy
just like the shepherds long ago.

Could you fail to see the star?
Colour of mica, silver, tinselled!
Pinned up there above the house,
look, a star, pinned right above!

I feel no joy, no envy – like
a saw's teeth cutting through my heart –
I look: what can I can give your son?
Here, take my cloak – my staff as well.

December 6th 1921

(2)

Clothed in his infant tears
as in a precious chasuble –
you, blessèd amongst women!
    Blessèd!

Opening his little eyes
where two roads form a cross.
(The other, too, an orphan –
son without a father.)

Clothed in his infant tears
as in a precious chasuble –
you, blessèd in your tears!
Blessèd!

Untroubled, pure, your forehead
while the fledgling sleeps –
a wreath of pealing church bells
formed a bed for you.

You, like a tree trembling
above the fledgling's sleep,
fathered by pealing church bells –
Virgin, celebrate!

In his snows beyond the clouds
as in a precious chasuble –
you, blessèd amongst snows!
Blessèd.

(3)

Sweep of an outsize wing,
breath coming like a lash:
– you, blessèd amongst women,
amongst all those who live.

Who brought the news? Storm, whiteness.
A whirling wind? A wing?
Who brought the news? Snow buried
both the news and the wing.

December 9th 1921

(4)

How to recompense you, how to help?
Blest to eternity! The infant's mother!

Bending over a transparent veil,
proclaiming once more: a light in the East!

From his blue eyes to the starry blue
you throw a bridge that takes a rainbow's form!

====

No danger of me falling! I can float!
Like a rainbow – bridge across the Neva.

Giver of new life in the hour of death!
Founder of empires! Mother to the son!

Grim song of his last, suffering gasp –
you set a firstborn down – 'He's here!'

December 10th 1921

(5)

With him to the end
in the final collapse:
what was there need of?
What name did they use?

Above a black ditch,
a combat of weeds,
the ultimate glory,
nameless – you arise.

He called: I can't breathe! Your unfailing: Friend!
Last of his women, still holding his hand!

With him to the end –
acclaimed by God's hosts.
Look, she's the one
who gave him to drink.

End of the relay
at his royal gates.
You kissed the froth
from his blue lips.

You kissed away the sweat his spasm brought.
He called: A hand to hold! You: Here it is!

With him to the end,
last to be close,
hugging him tight…

Tossing paradise into
the panic of his dying gaze.

Sung liturgy as veil,
the ultimate glory,
head covered, you proceed.

Trampling the commandments' arrogance,
when he gasped 'Mama!' you answered 'I'm here!'

December 11th 1921

Incontrovertible, so simple
it comes close to killing you –
two birds wove my nest – one was
the truth, the other orphanhood.

1921–1922

Eyebrows darting leagues apart.
Twin pledges of different loves –
black ruts that show me where to go –
your eyebrows' roads leading far off!

Hands raised, white willows in your wake.
Twin pledges of different partings,
bloodshed, but no tears are shed!
Life in blowing winds! Your eyebrows!

Swan's arrows of the chronicles.
Twin pledges of the White cause,
a rainbow – cast into a struggle
that belongs to God – your eyebrows!

January 23rd 1922

What's this – what wing, what sound
troubling my light sleep?
Where the quiet Don flows
a white swan in a fight.

What's this – bullet, a groan
making me clench my teeth?
Where the quiet Don flows
swans in combat: 'Marina!'

A forehead hits stone slabs.
At once I spread my wings.
A female falcon, pointed
wings – swans need my help!

People, snowstorm, help me
speed on over Moscow!
A female raven, pointed
wings – death by the Don!

His call: 'Marina!' Who
goes to meet the dawn,
my name, and clothed in white?
See him beyond that sea –
a white swan – and unharmed!

Greetings, Saint Yegoriy!
Swans engaged in combat!
See them, beyond the sea –
mine – and they're unharmed!

February 18th 1922

Acquaintance! Where did you reach these parts from?
Which wind are we to curse?
Acquaintance! I won't fall in love with you:
you look too like a thief.

For as long as a thief's fire keeps blazing,
a beauty's eyes will sparkle!
Acquaintance! Your delight's indulging whims,
while mine is saying "no".

Moscow, March 18th 1922

In the chapel they'd
abandoned I became
three – I fell as incense,
grain, flame on that forehead,

merged with birds' nocturnal
screech – on equal terms.
For you I shall be
miniature brazier,

domestic utensils,
smoke bad thoughts away,
chase tedium at night,
warm up earthly hands!

Gods cast me without pity
from their arms – so be it!
Love was assigned to me,
any love – so immense!

Think of the paths I trod!
And of the privileges!
Half my life? All for you!
Arm in arm? Here is mine!

Because you are in need,
because things torture you,
because hands here on earth
suffer calamity…

Pointless! There's no way of
adjusting amphibrachs!
Open your eyes wider,
look deep inside me,

not as Logos, not
as Infinity
did I arrive in your
arms, bare-headed, a

bird chirping...
           – Not to hold
sway! Wordless, loving you
on my word... Swallow with
the world's widest spread wings!

Berlin, June 26th 1922

And you say:
Wasn't it her,
wasn't it you
who through fingers:
leaves, flowers –
upon the sands...
           From oral
faiths – a Hindu,
turning our sadness –
into leaves,
our cargo – into flowers,
all so a hand might slip
into
a hand:
a game.
A Hindu, perhaps a Chrysostom
of faiths – with no eternity,

of willow trees with no
roots,
a forever – with no days…

(More wretched still
than you!)
So here,
about her,
only her.

July 3rd 1922

Could these be leaves, falling from trees,
from rose bushes, from a tea grove?
But no, her silken chasubles
are of pale, unpretentious brown…

Could these be twigs, inclining towards
water, algae and mouldering?
But no, arms she lets fall aspire
to nothing, and they have no soul.

Resins spilling out upon
the grass of fields that cuckoos haunt?
But no, these tears fell from her cheeks
on rugs – boring, don't you agree?

Your Honour's not concerned with this –
but just look at the brightening sky!
Amidst ruins of memories
day breaking for her in his eyes!

<1922>

Divine, without restraint,
breakers as they swell –
not lips greedily pressed
onto an alien hand –

silent toil of a shell
when the tide's on the ebb –
divine, without restraint
their singing of the sea.

<1922>

Imperceptibly the golden
strands of my hair are turning grey.
– No regretting! It all happened,
merged and sang inside of me.

Combined in song – like all that's distant
in the suburb siren's groan.
Dear God: a soul learned to be –
that was your most secret plan.

=============

Salt of my speculations fire
could not consume – should I exchange
those phoenix ashes for the tar
of splendours that will quickly fade?

But you, too, fellow traveller,
turned silver! To thunder and fumes,
young locks that *actions* coloured grey –
my thoughts' parables with their grey.

Flower of gold, so self-conceited,
don't get puffed up with your lushness:
young locks *calamities* turned grey
suit laurels, and the civil oak.

between September 17th and 23rd 1922

And what of love? A shepherd lad
beating on his downturned palm,
an earthquake that's three seconds long
on the mountains of Paradise.

Those infernos and those heavens,
abysses and soaring flights –
mere transitory poles supporting
weightless iron couplings.

I ate my fill! – My teeth would grind
fleeting moments whole years long,
seen in a dream, a heart that plunges
to the gullet's very depths.

Fairytales we read at school!
The ode we're looking for soars high,
its target not laughter, but death:
mountains that are genuine!

September 29th 1922

Orphaned air beyond the grave,
migrants on their way…
Quivering of orphaned wires,
rails making their way back…

As though my life had been dispatched
along those leagues of steel –
an orphaned mist – twin distances –
(Moscow, a curtsey here!)

As though I were being put to death,
exiting my last veins,
an orphaned mist, down those two veins
my life ebbing away.

October 28th 1922

ASRAEL

Not delighting at my hand's touch,
shedding not a tear between my arms,
more definite and incontrovertible
than a torch that's been turned upside down:

bending over my soul at the bed's head
or, at its foot, over my drudgery
(not shrinking away when my hand came close –
yours was not the hand deposing me) –

Asrael! On moonless nights, when stars
are absent, along paths that have been scythed,
in the weighty hour that needs such effort,
I won't be a weight for you to bear...

Asrael? On nights with no way out,
when stars are absent and masks torn away,
in the hour when breathing's such an effort
I won't be a bottomless pit for you...

Later, with your finger as a torch,
write the story, in the greying dawns,
of a woman who, rather than call
you Asrael, chose Eros as your name.

February 17th 1923

A font for doves,
the sky: the world's far end.

I, having strolled beyond the seas,
feel stifled in a one-night room
by your arms,
by your lips,
yes, you – and by
your sirens, city!
       City!
In me forty times
forty domes are singing.
Forty smiths –
such shattering blows –
hammering inside me!
I, more used to deciding in marble,
feel stifled in a one-night room
by Love and by Democracy.

March 21st 1923

PRAGUE

Where dates get mixed up, buildings get entangled
in blue air, street numbers are not for real!
Let me speak of my portentous life
in a city so resembling Lethe.

Let me speak of how it slept, but not
as much as it would like to – stretched its outline
where river weeds meet opal, and the day
rejoices like a Virgin by the bridges.

Where past sleeping Madonnas and past knights
with lifted eyebrows, one step at a time,
a population of descendants hurries
onwards in whom that same blood survives,

where honour, calling out and brandishing
the last swords, did not linger in the row.
A city where everything gazes at you
through the eyes of the last of the stock.

April 21st 1923

NIGHT

When we lie to each other
(night passed off as day)
when we hunt for each other
(word passed off as essence)

when we cling to each other
prostrate and deluded
(pitch passed off as linen,
fire passed off as smoke)

come to me in the night

like this: a Maytime bug,
summer midnight falsehood
or else: night's dark iris
passed off as an eyelid…

Do you think night was shy
and departed at dawn?
Like this: night's dark iris
passed off as an eyelid…

Light is merely flesh!
A stylite at the crossroads.
Light – a sort of sheepskin
essence has thrown on.

A river underground –
God – night in the light…
Like this: night's dark iris
passed off as an eyelid…

Do you think the gaze
vanished? Lift it! It flows!
Light is merely weight,
merely totalling up…

Light – merely an eyelid
hiding chaos…

Do you think night
is shy?
A river underground,
that's night – deep under day!

– Enough! Let me depart
into night's fiery river.

Light – merely an eyelid
hiding chaos…

When we delude each other
(words curtaining the depths!)
when we honour each other,
when we love each other…

June 1923

LOTUS JUICE

A divine forehead, naked like a child,
glimmers in the shadows of the tropics.
Eyes steadfastly cast down bespeak a shyness
that's only found in the best families.

In writings that a young girl left behind,
scarlet offshoot, you provoke my wonder,
whose virginity is intertwined
with impeccable manners, as with creepers.

Prolong your saintliness! Watch over lips
and eyes, those sacrosanct receptacles!
Love itself was born beneath the tropics,
that's the place I journeyed from to you:

out of ferns and tangled undergrowth,
out of reedbeds, paths no one can trace…
There total and utter oblivion
comes to a halt upon the outstretched palm

of a lotus stalk. The juice inclines you
to sleep. A wine that generates no froth,
that's lotus juice. Lotus juice provokes
a sort of faintness in the limbs of children

and women... Look, the palm is empty now.
At the hour when in the East the moon
emerges (lotus juice), from lips to lips
learn the taste of sleep – of lotus juice.

July 23rd 1923

Just like into the seas' pure blue –
the eyes of tragic heroines.
In this hall, boundless, entry free,
eyes of Ariadnes, sleeping
and abandoned, of rejected
Phaedras invoking in vain
a knife from deep inside their guts...
I look inside me: Still alive?

July 24th 1923

However bitter, gulping down the smoke
your chimneys belch out offers me such bliss!
Seeing that the city, when night falls,
might make you think the sky's turned upside down.

However stark the day of your despicable
activities, night makes of you – a shah!
Passion has brought the stars down onto earth!
Constellations are mapped out in the dust.

What name am I to call you? Bonaparte
or Hector? Are you Moscow, or else Troy?
There lies the city, mapping constellations
and battlefields...
                    Love? – A mere bagatelle!

It passes! Protégé of otherworldly
indigence, night makes of me – a shah!
The heavens have been brought down to the earth,
constellations mapped out in a dust that

scatters…

August 30th 1923

Along the riverbanks, grey trees show where
Ophelia passed… (She took her necklace off
so as not to die in her best clothes!)
And nonetheless
(for us, the bier is preferable
to being undesired!
Unbearable even
when dead, though we may carry
mountains on our hearts older than time!) –
she weaved together all
her few springs – floated onwards,
betrothed and garlanded.

A not unselfish
victim to the world:
Ophelia – her leaves,
Orpheus – his lyre…
What about me?

September 28th 1923

EYE

Streetlamps where the gas flames burn
as day by day it gets more freezing.
Streetlamps that gaze like eyes – I still
can't work out what they blame us for.
Streetlamps that gaze down on the earth,
on infant children, and on me.

October 23rd 1923

You, who loved me with the lie
of truth, and with the truth of lies.
You, who loved me to the utmost
limit – even went beyond!

You who loved me longer than
time lasts – a wave of the right hand!
You just don't love me any more:
seven words – the unvarnished truth.

December 12th 1923

Pillars in a throne room that's
abandoned (in the nick of time!)
Streets descending steeply with
the impetuousness of brooks.

Feelings, maddened honeysuckle,
lips whose call blots memories out.
That's how I tumbled from your arms
into the stormy seas of stanzas.

December 1923

Song from a wound between the prince's ribs.
Or, in his wound, was it an arrow

sang? – No way of reaching the beloved
(it sang), so as to say his funeral rite
(it sang). Winging its way across the dove-
blue steppes. – Or was it just the steppes
that sang, washing a white
corpse clean…? "My swan, wild goose of mine",
it sang. Sang, stretching to the Don
from the blue Danube…
      Maybe Russia
sang?

December 30th 1924

Not thundering from passing wheels –
the two of us shot glances at each other.

Not Babel's tower come tumbling down –
we two proved our souls were equal in strength.

Not a Pacific hurricane –
two Scythians shooting arrows at each other.

January 16th 1925

Days that resemble crawling slugs…
My days are spent in stitching lines…
What do I care about my life?
It can't be mine if it's not yours.

And my calamities? What do
I care about them? Eating? Sleeping?
Or care about this mortal body?
It can't be mine if it's not yours

January 1925

Arrogance – a matter of caste.
Something runs short – you'll do without.
Comments are pointless. So infrequent!
Occurs once every thousand years.

All that I said – a cry while going
under, signal to the sailors!
The rest remained a mystery
they'll cut out along with my tongue.

May 16th 1925

Fame falls, plopping just like a plum –
onto your head, into your skirt.
To be happy, and beautiful!
(The words feel inappropriate –

"to be"? With nothing else tacked on?
"To be". A full stop. Then a space.)
Fame falls as the word "mercy" falls
upon the executioner's axe,

or else, on flagstones in a church,
it falls at midday, like dry rain.
To be happy, and celebrated?
Our deadlines don't extend that far.

Or else it falls like all of Rome
onto the branches of a rose.
– Fame! – I had no time for you:
I couldn't have put up with you.

May 17th 1925

From native villages!
– Mirages! Things no-one has seen before!
Just chugging on and on,
a train that wouldn't stop at any station,

no final terminus!
To what's ancient! Never been built upon!
Buffeted by the wind,
as if it were a beater made from straw,

brain growing fresh and chill –
settling in a rut, it got so mouldy! –
A train bearing its load
more quickly than a swan, like in the ditty…

A sea squall on dry land!
Barriers crashing down! Without restraint!
Train darting on and on,
with not even the hint of a delay.

Not getting stuck! Crucial!
Swearing no oaths, never getting sated!
Whistling without a pause,
above the curse of ordinary doings.

Cornfields of bygone days!
Primordial clods! Things no hand ever soiled!
Train hissing without end,
it would never get time to look around

on places it belonged,
arid and puffed up with their own importance!
Pest, Brest – where's the difference?
It would never get time to lend an ear,

or else to sleep. To sleep?! –
Last, most unjustifiable of sins…
Birds flying in reverse,
following the tracks of falling trees!

Not one night, not two! – Two?! –
Still further on, beyond a certain empire.
One I'd never get off,
the train that would be bringing me to you.

end of May 1925

from POEMS TO BLOK (1922)

10

See him – look there! – grown tired of foreign parts,
leader, no men,

drinking with cupped hand from a mountain stream,
prince with no land.

There he has all he needs, kingdom and troops,
mother and bread.

Legislate for your wondrous heritage,
unfriended friend!

August 15th 1921

11

For us you will remain a monk,
a darling one, good-looking too,
a breviary written by hand,
a small casket of cypress wood.

For all women, with no exceptions,
those who are swallows, us with garlands,
those who are grey and us, still gold,
son to every one of us.

For us you will remain the firstborn,
the son who left or was turned out,
our walking-stick along the roads,
our pilgrim when the day is young.

All of us searching for a cross
with a brief inscription in the
Smolensk graveyard, queuing up,
all of us <...> unbelieving.

Son to us all, inheritor,
our Alpha and our Omega.

August 15th 1921

12

Friends of his, don't trouble him!
Servants of his, leave him in peace!
The writing on his face was clear:
  "My kingdom is not of this world."

Prophetic snowstorms coursed his veins,
his wings' weight made his shoulders curve,
he dropped his soul, just like a swan,
into parched dust, a singing cleft!

Weighty bronze, just fall, just fall!
Wings learned they had the right to fly!
Lips calling out the word "Respond"'
knew that dying does not exist.

Drinking dawns and seas, carousing
although sated. No funeral rites!
There will be bread enough for one
whose timeless order was: "Exist!"

August 15th 1921

13

Over the plains –
cry of a swan.
How could you fail to recognise
your son? From far beyond the clouds
it reaches us – his last farewell.

Over the plains –
fateful snowstorms.
How could you fail to recognise
your partner? Bloodstained wings, vestments
in tatters – and his last "live on!"

Over the sinner –
dazzling wings.
God's envoy snatched a soul – praise be!
The convict found a warm bed, the
stepson his mother's home – Amen.

between August 15th and 25th 1921

14

It wasn't ribs that cracked –
a wing has snapped right through.

No firing squad transfixed
his chest. You can't extract

that bullet. Wings don't mend.
He walks lop-sided now.

===============

His chain a garland made from blackthorns!
Dead, what can a mob's convulsions

mean to him, the swan's down of
a woman's flattery? Unhearing,

he went alone, transmuting sunsets
to ice with statues' eyeless orbs.

The only thing alive in him
a wing that had been snapped right through.

between August 15th and 21st 1921

15

Without a call, without a sound –
roofworker slipping from a roof –
but maybe you're already back.
Could you be lying in a cradle?

Incandescent, not growing dim,
light source only a few weeks old…
Among women fated to die
which is the one that rocks your cradle?

Most fortunate of burdens! Reed
singing forth its prophecies!
Who is going to let me know
which is the cradle where you lie?

"As long as he's not been betrayed!"
Filled with protective jealousy
I make a circuit to the furthest
corners of this Russian land.

Traversing regions midnight rules
from one to the other extreme,
I seek his mouth, that parting wound,
those two blue eyes the hue of lead.

To catch hold of him! Clutch him tight!
To give him love, and still more love!
Who's going to whisper news to me
about the cradle where you lie?

Small delicate grains of pearls,
a muslin canopy for sleep,
a crown of blackthorn, not of laurel,
sharp-pointed shadow of his cap.

No bed-curtain, instead a bird
has spread its two white wings out wide?
Was he reborn so driving snow
could blow in blizzards yet again?

To seize him, run away with him!
Higher! Hold on! Don't let him go!
Who's going to breathe news to me
about the cradle where you lie?

My efforts could be pointless, though,
my enterprise a huge mistake.
Now that you're underneath the ground,
you may sleep till the trumpet sounds.

Once more I contemplate the massive
cavities that were your temples.
Someone as tired as this cannot
be wakened even with a trumpet!

Pastures of the utmost power,
rusting silence filled with hope.
The guard's the one who'll let me know
which is the cradle where you lie.

November 22nd 1921

16

Sleepy, as if drunken,
taken unawares.
The chasms of those temples –
conscience that does not sleep.

Eye sockets abandoned,
gleaming still in death.
The visionary prophet's
an empty pane of glass.

Was it not you
who couldn't bear the rustling
of her tunic
returning up the gorge from Hades?

Was it not yours,
the head replete with jingling
silver that bobbed
down the Hebrus' sleepy waters?

November 25th 1921

17

Therefore, oh Lord! accept my coin
for establishing your church.
I'm singing of my homeland's wound,
not of my own unbridled loving,

not of some skinflint's rusting coffers,
or granite knees have worn away…
Returned to all, hero and tsar,
exemplary singer death took,

he flows towards you, Russia, down
the Dnieper, breaking up the ice
at Eastertide. No need to trouble
coffin planks, thousand-voiced flood!

Shed tears, then, heart, and sing forth praise!
Let mortal love be jealous of
your wail that mingles with a thousand.
That other delights in the chorus.

December 7th 1921

from THE CRAFT (1922)

BETHLEHEM

*(two poems which somehow didn't
find their way into the* Poems to Blok*)*

to Blok's son, Sasha

1

Not with silver I came,
not with amber I came,
not as an emperor,
but as a shepherd girl.

Bringing air from my hills,
the piercing gaze of my
two eyes – and the red blaze
of my fires and dawns.

No incense, no wax? Fur?
Not ashamed of my rags!
Maybe poorest of all –
that means I take first place!

One camel, another
climbing up your steep hill.
Look: emperors arriving.
Look: carrying chests.

They – are – too – late!

November 23rd 1921

2

Emperors three,
bearing three chests,
inside them precious gifts.

In the first –
the whole earth –
with all its blue seas.

In the next –
Noah's freight,
animals in the ark.

And the third?
What's in there?
Emperor, what have you there?

Gives his gift,
dearest God!
No way of telling what!

He moves close,
and the mother
flinches, the child weeps.

November 23rd 1921

NOTES

These notes are intended to complement the introduction. Information given there is not duplicated here.

Darling fellow travellers we shared a
Tsvetaeva subsequently replaced 'Frantic horses neighing' with 'The raging wind' and then 'The morning wind'.

Knight in the image of an angel
The word translated here as 'keyholder' strictly means the person entrusted with care of the vestments and objects required for rites in an Orthodox church.

Courage, virginity, a combination
'World' here could also be rendered 'peace', as the two words are identical in Russian.

Lyrics from the Play 'The Disciple'
A later version of the closing stanzas of 8 runs as follows:

> Sooner or later, you'll observe
> the sea's currents from on board ship
> and say: 'I fell in love with a
> girl of the seas – who drowned in them!
>
> Could it be yours, that silver tail
> glimpsed among the coral trees –
> daughter carried in no mother's
> womb, but in the sea's?'

To the Jews
The reference in the fourth stanza is to Heinrich Heine (1797–1856), a fundamental influence on Tsvetaeva's lyrical output.

I picture you with dark eyes – Separation!
The second stanza refers to the moment in Tolstoy's novel when, having left her husband, Anna Karenina looks in on her sleeping son. Stenka Razin was a leader of Cossack rebels in 17th century Russia.

Hair like short wings, a flurry was inspired by Lann, together with a wooden image of Paganini by the sculptor Sergey Konenkov (1874–1971), known as 'the Russian Rodin'. Tsvetaeva quotes from a conversation she had about Lann in her letter to him of December 6th 1920: "'I liked him a lot. And did you notice, he's exactly like Konenkov's Paganini – he could have modelled for it!" Me, livening up: "I've never seen Konenkov's Paganini, I'm shortsighted, but – how peculiar – the first time we met, within ten minutes of him arriving, I told him he resembled Paganini'".

Competition's scab did not
Presumably inspired by false rumours about Akhmatova's death.

www.ingramcontent.com/pod-product-compliance
Lightning Source LLC
Chambersburg PA
CBHW031401160426
43196CB00007B/846